T0084155

GRAPHIC BIOGRAPHIES

# MOTHER JONES
## LABOR LEADER

by Connie Colwell Miller

illustrated by Steve Erwin and
Charles Barnett III

Consultant:
Leslie F. Orear
President
Illinois Labor History Society
Chicago, Illinois

Capstone
press
Mankato, Minnesota

Graphic Library is published by Capstone Press,
1710 Roe Crest Drive, North Mankato, Minnesota 56003.
capstonepub.com



*Library of Congress Cataloging-in-Publication Data*

Miller, Connie Colwell, 1976–

Mother Jones : labor leader / by Connie Colwell Miller ; illustrated by Steve Erwin and Charles Barnett III.

p. cm. — (Graphic library. Graphic biographies)

Includes bibliographical references and index.

Summary: "In graphic novel format, tells the story of Mary "Mother" Jones, a leading labor union and child labor activist in the late 1800s and early 1900s"—Provided by publisher.

ISBN-13: 978-0-7368-5487-0 (hardcover)
ISBN-10: 0-7368-5487-8 (hardcover)
ISBN-13: 978-0-7368-9662-7 (softcover pbk.)
ISBN-10: 0-7368-9662-7 (softcover pbk.)

1. Jones, Mother, 1843?–1930—Juvenile literature. 2. Women labor leaders—United States—Biography—Juvenile literature. 3. Labor unions—Organizing—United States—History—Juvenile literature. 4. Child labor—United States—History—Juvenile literature.
5. Women in the labor movement—United States—Biography—Juvenile literature. 6. Graphic novels. I. Erwin, Steve. II. Barnett, Charles, III. III. Title. IV. Series.
HD8073.J6M55 2007
331.88092—dc22 2006007302

*Art Direction and Design*
Bob Lentz

*Colorist*
Melissa Kaercher

*Editor*
Gillia Olson

**Editor's note:** Direct quotations from primary sources are indicated by a yellow background.

Direct quotations appear on the following pages:

Pages 7, 8, 11, 16, 26, from *The Autobiography of Mother Jones* by Mary "Mother" Jones (Chicago: C. H. Kerr for the Illinois Labor History Society, 1976).

Page 10 from *Mother Jones Speaks: Collected Writings and Speeches*, edited by Philip S. Foner (New York: Monad Press, 1983).

Page 17 from the *Philadelphia North American*, July 7, 1903, as quoted in *Mother Jones: The Most Dangerous Woman in America* by Elliott J. Gorn (New York: Hill and Wang, 2001).

Page 25: letter from Britt Adams to president Woodrow Wilson, as quoted in *Mother Jones: The Most Dangerous Woman in America* by Elliott J. Gorn (New York: Hill and Wang, 2001).

Printed in the United States 5499

# TABLE of CONTENTS

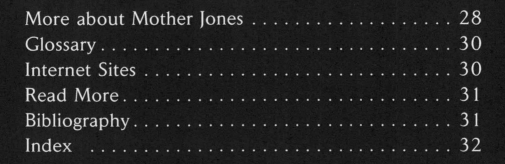

# Chapter 1
# WORKING CLASS STRUGGLES

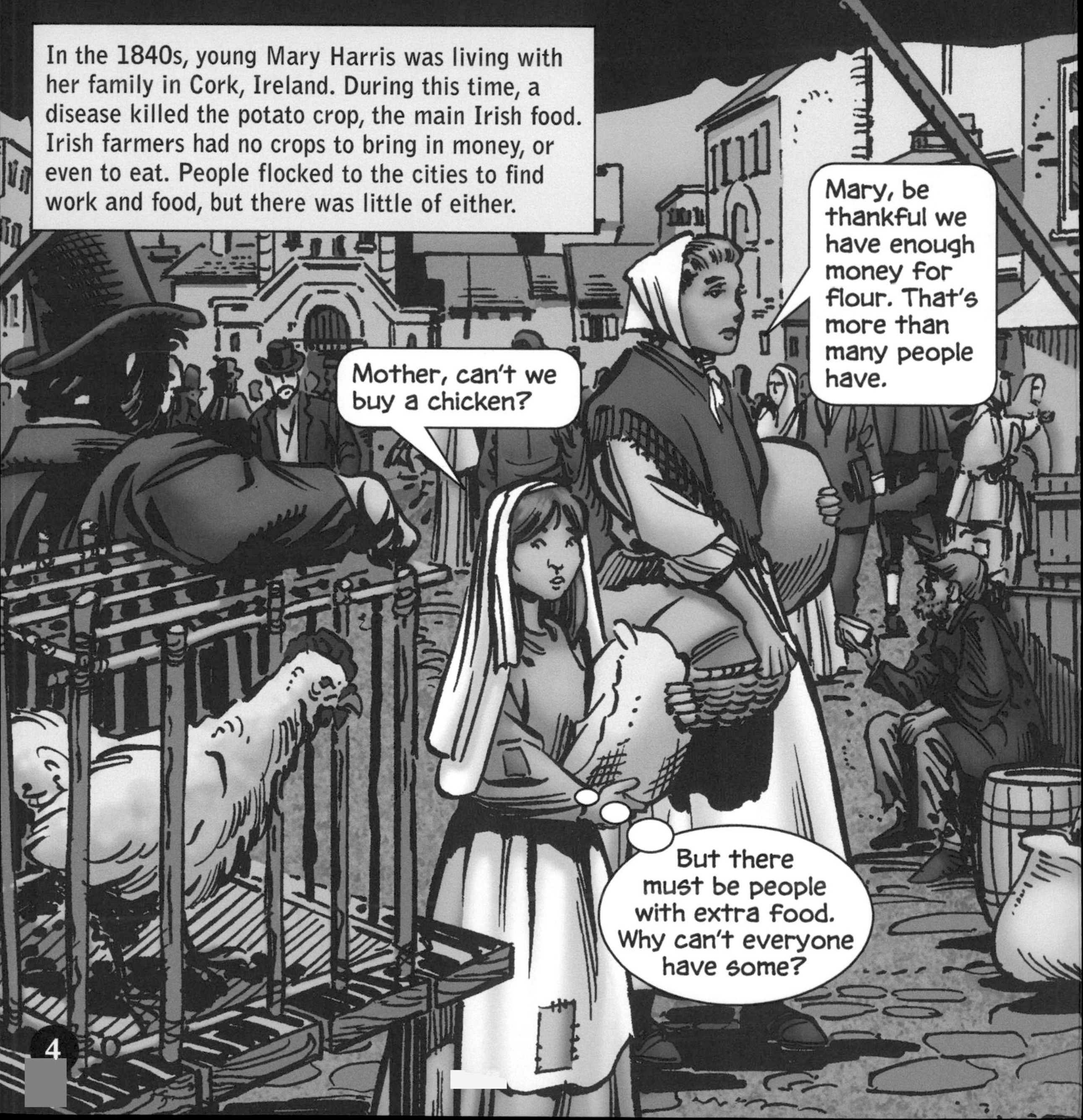
In the 1840s, young Mary Harris was living with her family in Cork, Ireland. During this time, a disease killed the potato crop, the main Irish food. Irish farmers had no crops to bring in money, or even to eat. People flocked to the cities to find work and food, but there was little of either.
Mother, can't we buy a chicken?
Mary, be thankful we have enough money for flour. That's more than many people have.
But there must be people with extra food. Why can't everyone have some?

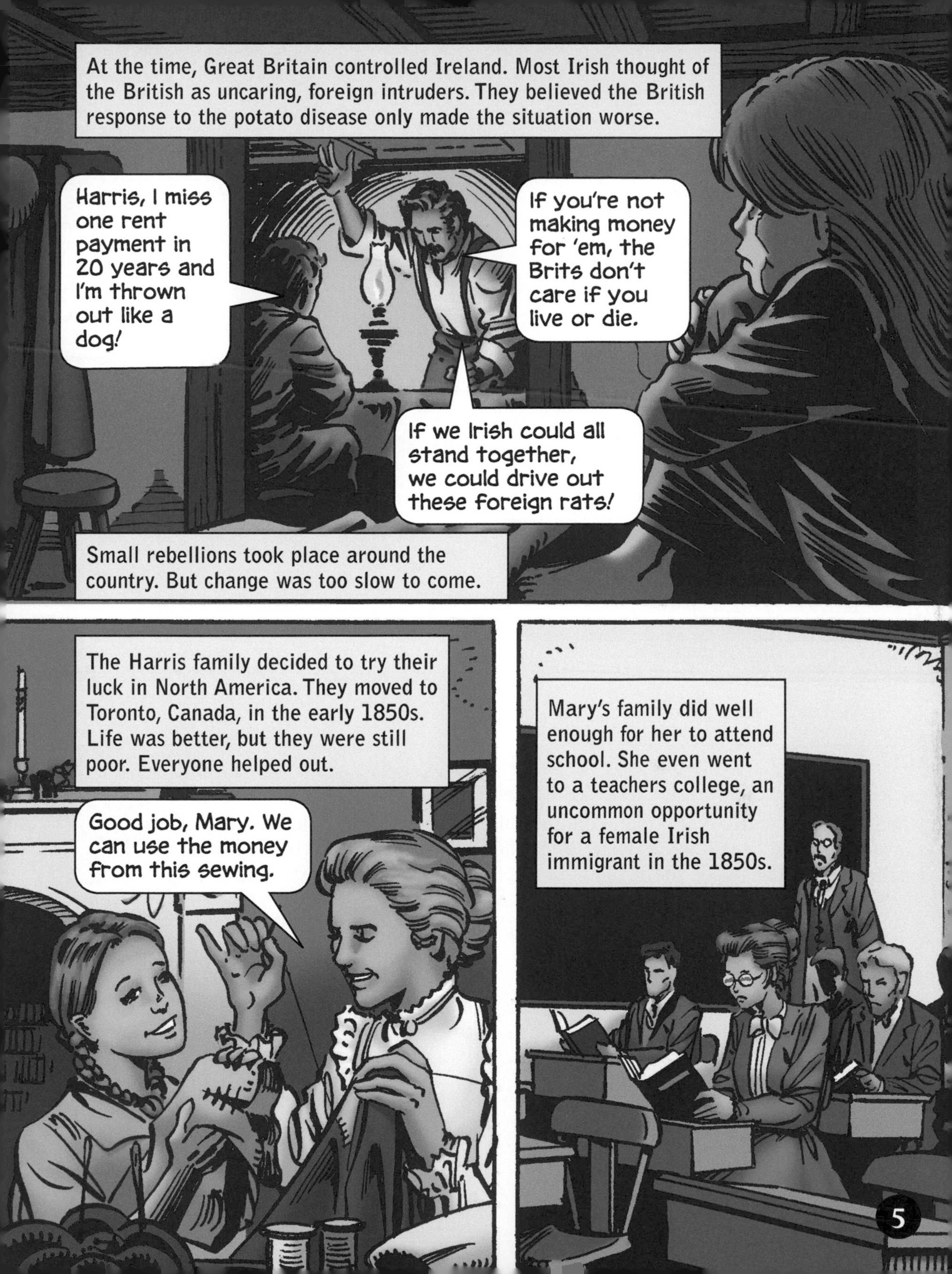
At the time, Great Britain controlled Ireland. Most Irish thought of the British as uncaring, foreign intruders. They believed the British response to the potato disease only made the situation worse.
Harris, I miss one rent payment in 20 years and I'm thrown out like a dog!
If you're not making money for 'em, the Brits don't care if you live or die.
If we Irish could all stand together, we could drive out these foreign rats!
Small rebellions took place around the country. But change was too slow to come.
The Harris family decided to try their luck in North America. They moved to Toronto, Canada, in the early 1850s. Life was better, but they were still poor. Everyone helped out.
Good job, Mary. We can use the money from this sewing.
Mary's family did well enough for her to attend school. She even went to a teachers college, an uncommon opportunity for a female Irish immigrant in the 1850s.

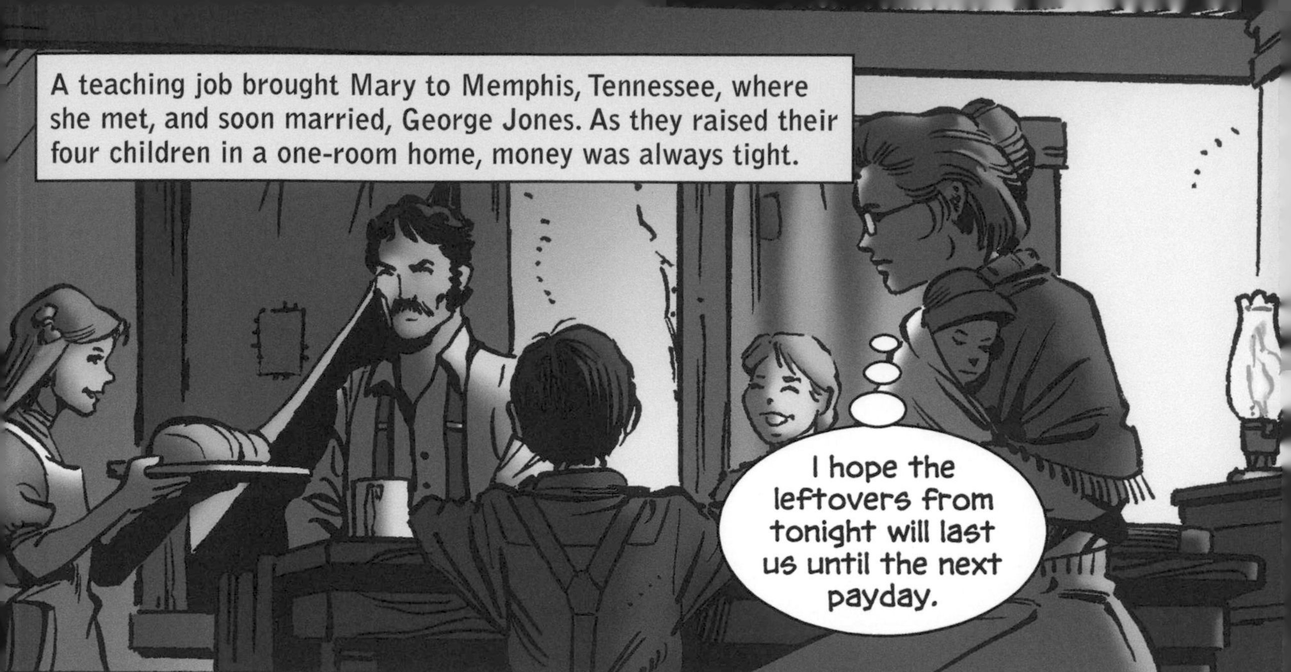
A teaching job brought Mary to Memphis, Tennessee, where she met, and soon married, George Jones. As they raised their four children in a one-room home, money was always tight.
I hope the leftovers from tonight will last us until the next payday.

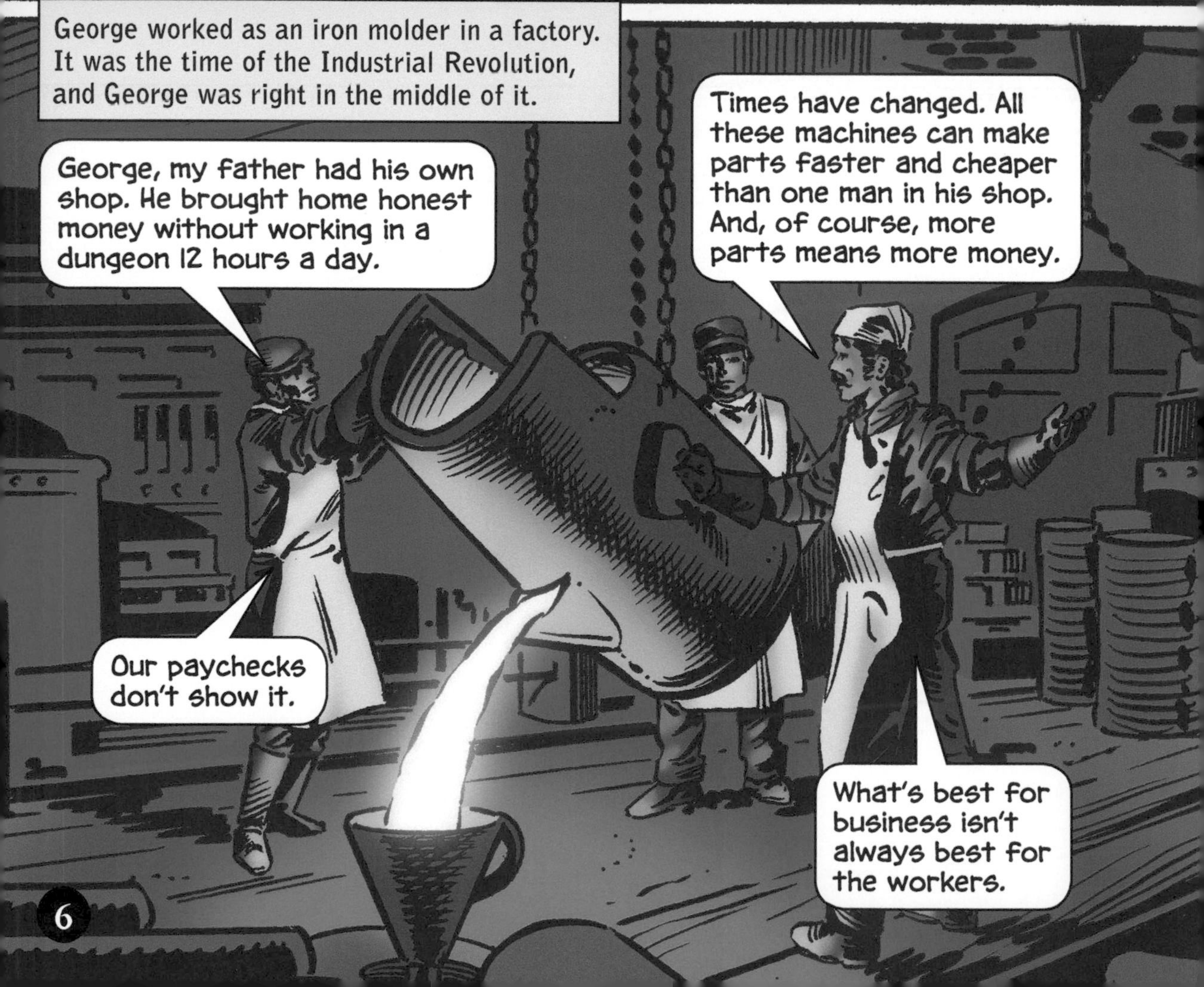
George worked as an iron molder in a factory. It was the time of the Industrial Revolution, and George was right in the middle of it.
George, my father had his own shop. He brought home honest money without working in a dungeon 12 hours a day.
Times have changed. All these machines can make parts faster and cheaper than one man in his shop. And, of course, more parts means more money.
Our paychecks don't show it.
What's best for business isn't always best for the workers.

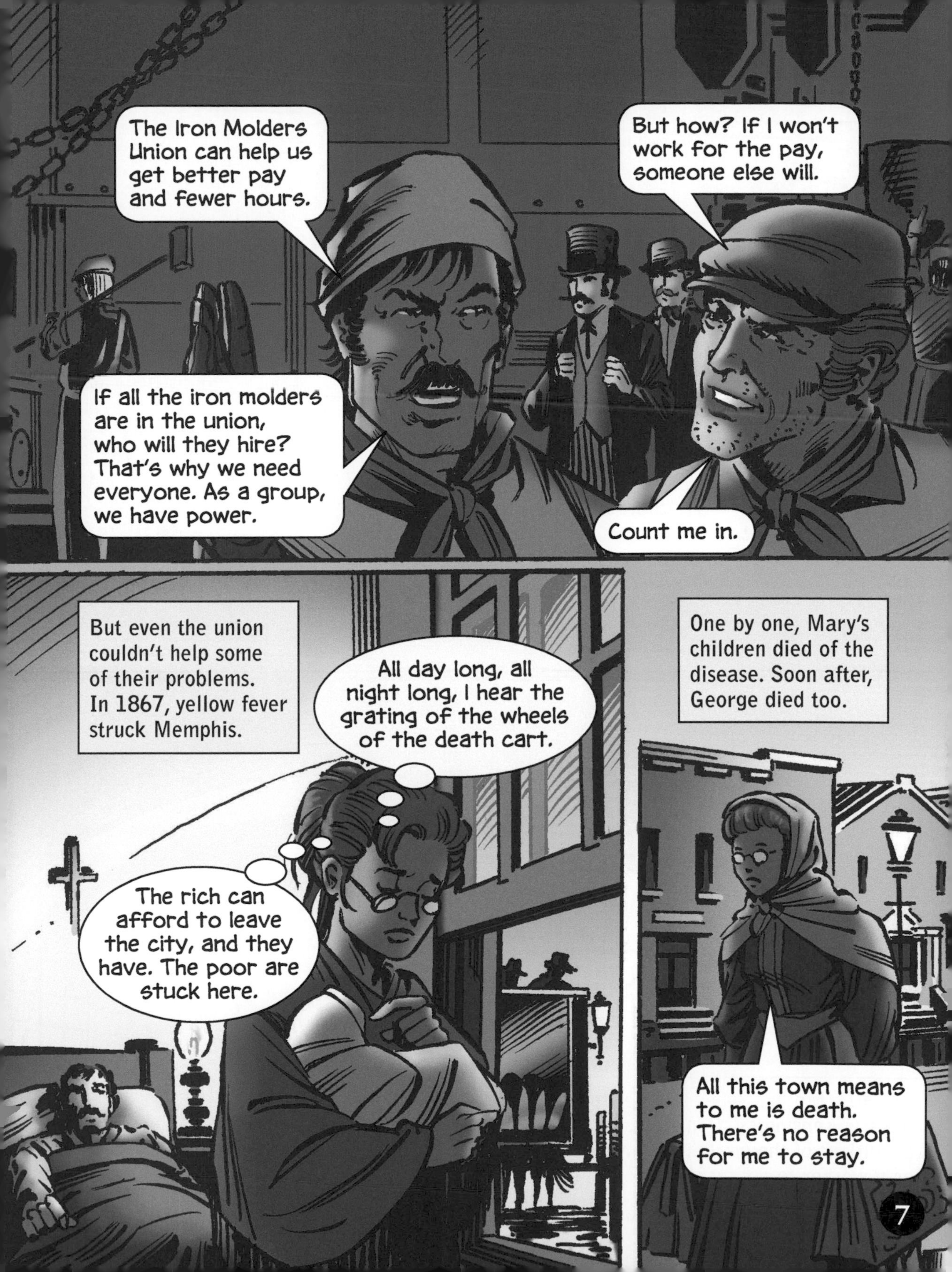
The Iron Molders Union can help us get better pay and fewer hours.
But how? If I won't work for the pay, someone else will.
If all the iron molders are in the union, who will they hire? That's why we need everyone. As a group, we have power.
Count me in.
But even the union couldn't help some of their problems. In 1867, yellow fever struck Memphis.
All day long, all night long, I hear the grating of the wheels of the death cart.
The rich can afford to leave the city, and they have. The poor are stuck here.
One by one, Mary's children died of the disease. Soon after, George died too.
All this town means to me is death. There's no reason for me to stay.

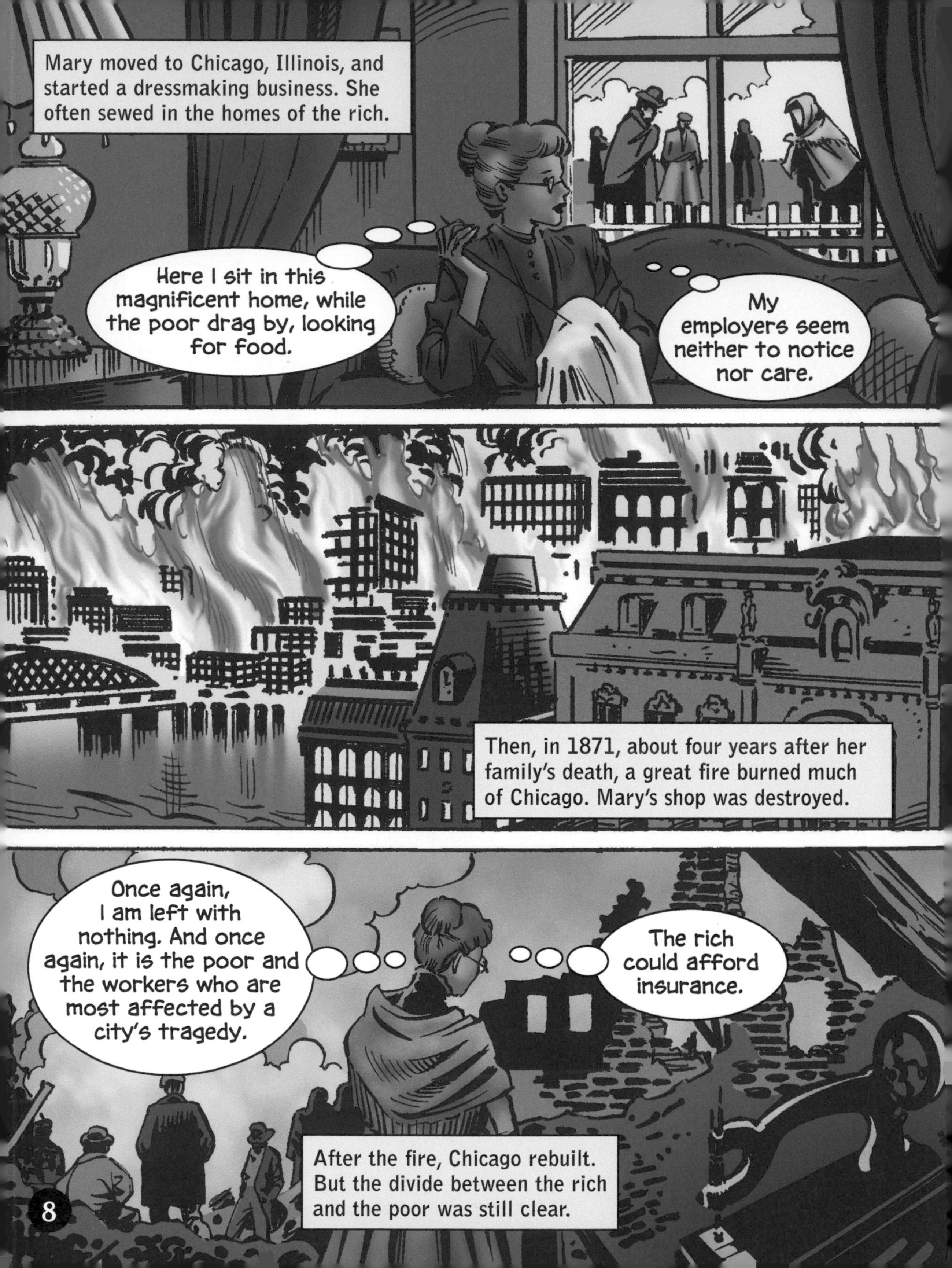
Mary moved to Chicago, Illinois, and started a dressmaking business. She often sewed in the homes of the rich.
Here I sit in this magnificent home, while the poor drag by, looking for food.
My employers seem neither to notice nor care.
Then, in 1871, about four years after her family's death, a great fire burned much of Chicago. Mary's shop was destroyed.
Once again, I am left with nothing. And once again, it is the poor and the workers who are most affected by a city's tragedy.
The rich could afford insurance.
After the fire, Chicago rebuilt. But the divide between the rich and the poor was still clear.

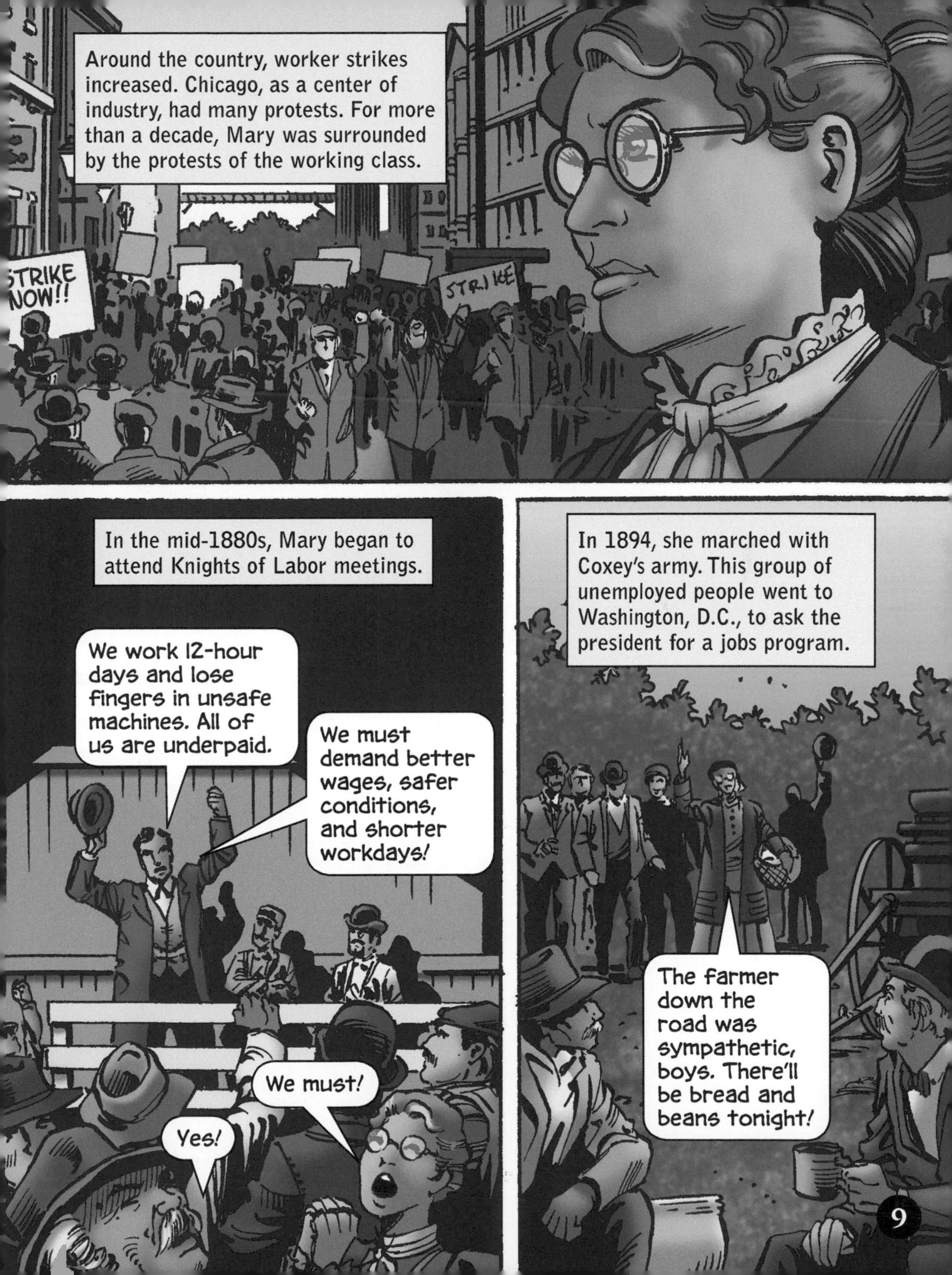
Around the country, worker strikes increased. Chicago, as a center of industry, had many protests. For more than a decade, Mary was surrounded by the protests of the working class.
STRIKE NOW!!
STRIKE
In the mid-1880s, Mary began to attend Knights of Labor meetings.
We work 12-hour days and lose fingers in unsafe machines. All of us are underpaid.
We must demand better wages, safer conditions, and shorter workdays!
We must!
Yes!
In 1894, she marched with Coxey's army. This group of unemployed people went to Washington, D.C., to ask the president for a jobs program.
The farmer down the road was sympathetic, boys. There'll be bread and beans tonight!

# Chapter 2
# MOPS AND MINERS' WIVES

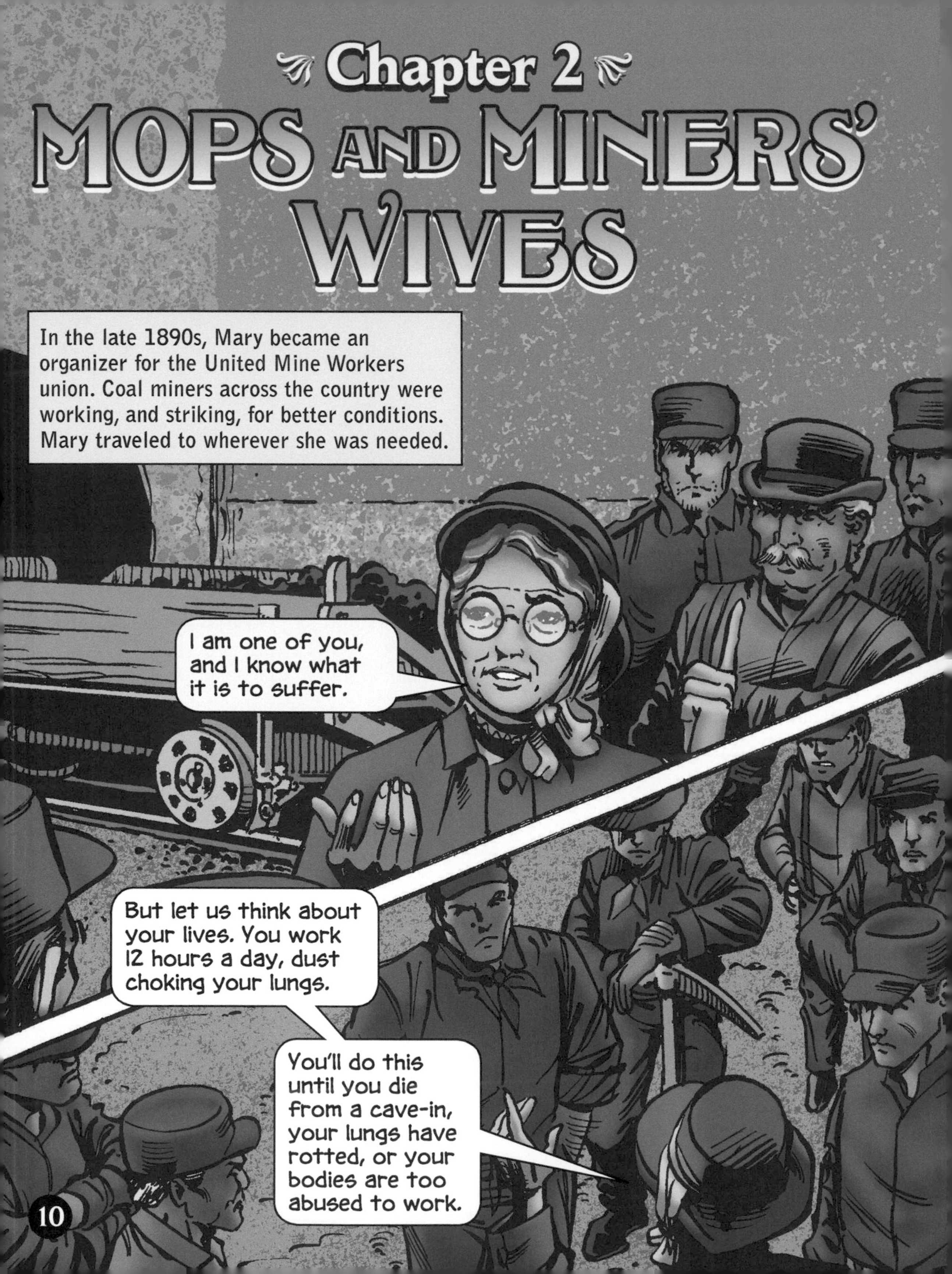
In the late 1890s, Mary became an organizer for the United Mine Workers union. Coal miners across the country were working, and striking, for better conditions. Mary traveled to wherever she was needed.
I am one of you, and I know what it is to suffer.
But let us think about your lives. You work 12 hours a day, dust choking your lungs.
You'll do this until you die from a cave-in, your lungs have rotted, or your bodies are too abused to work.

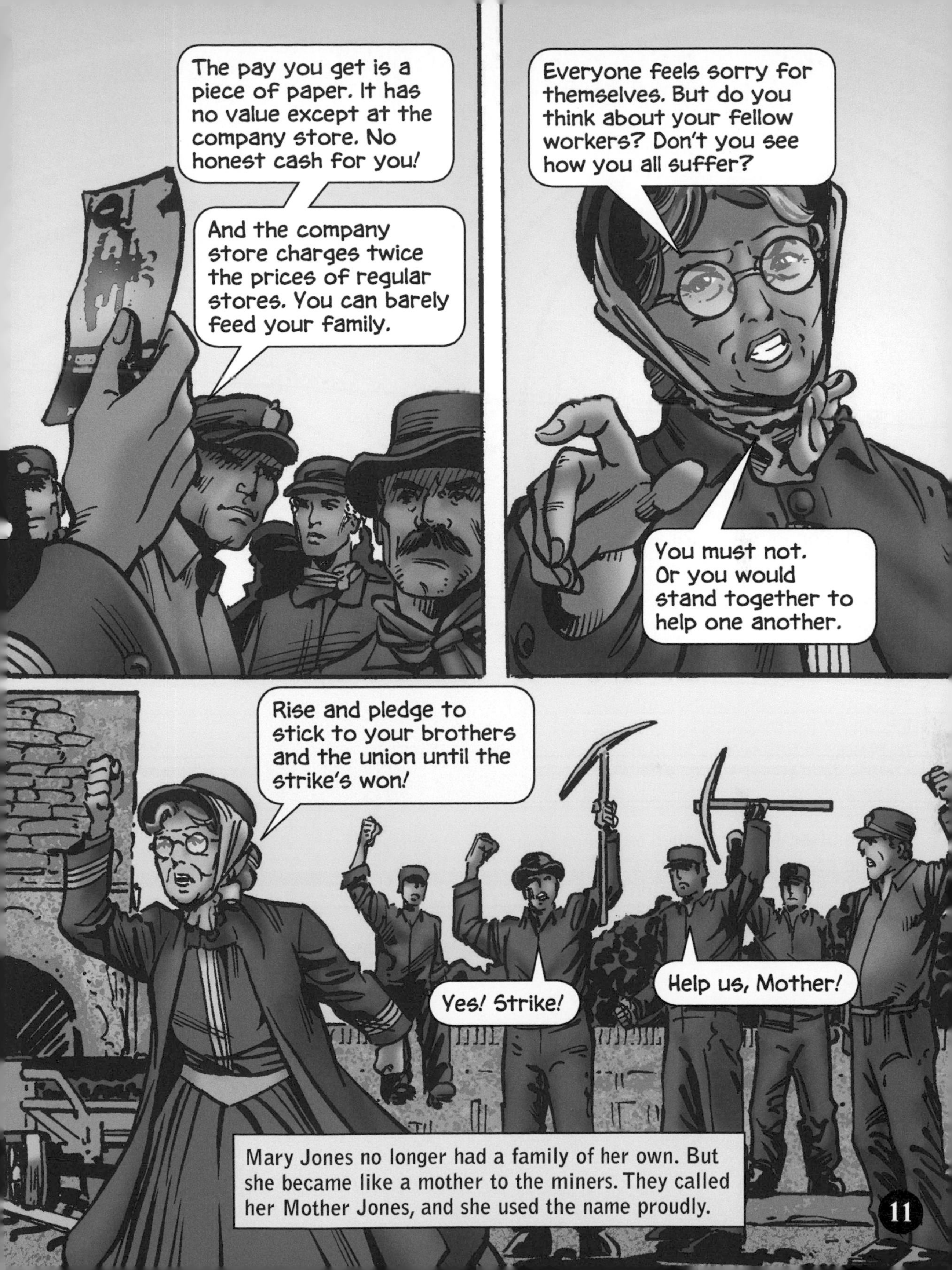
The pay you get is a piece of paper. It has no value except at the company store. No honest cash for you!
And the company store charges twice the prices of regular stores. You can barely feed your family.
Everyone feels sorry for themselves. But do you think about your fellow workers? Don't you see how you all suffer?
You must not. Or you would stand together to help one another.
Rise and pledge to stick to your brothers and the union until the strike's won!
Yes! Strike!
Help us, Mother!
Mary Jones no longer had a family of her own. But she became like a mother to the miners. They called her Mother Jones, and she used the name proudly.

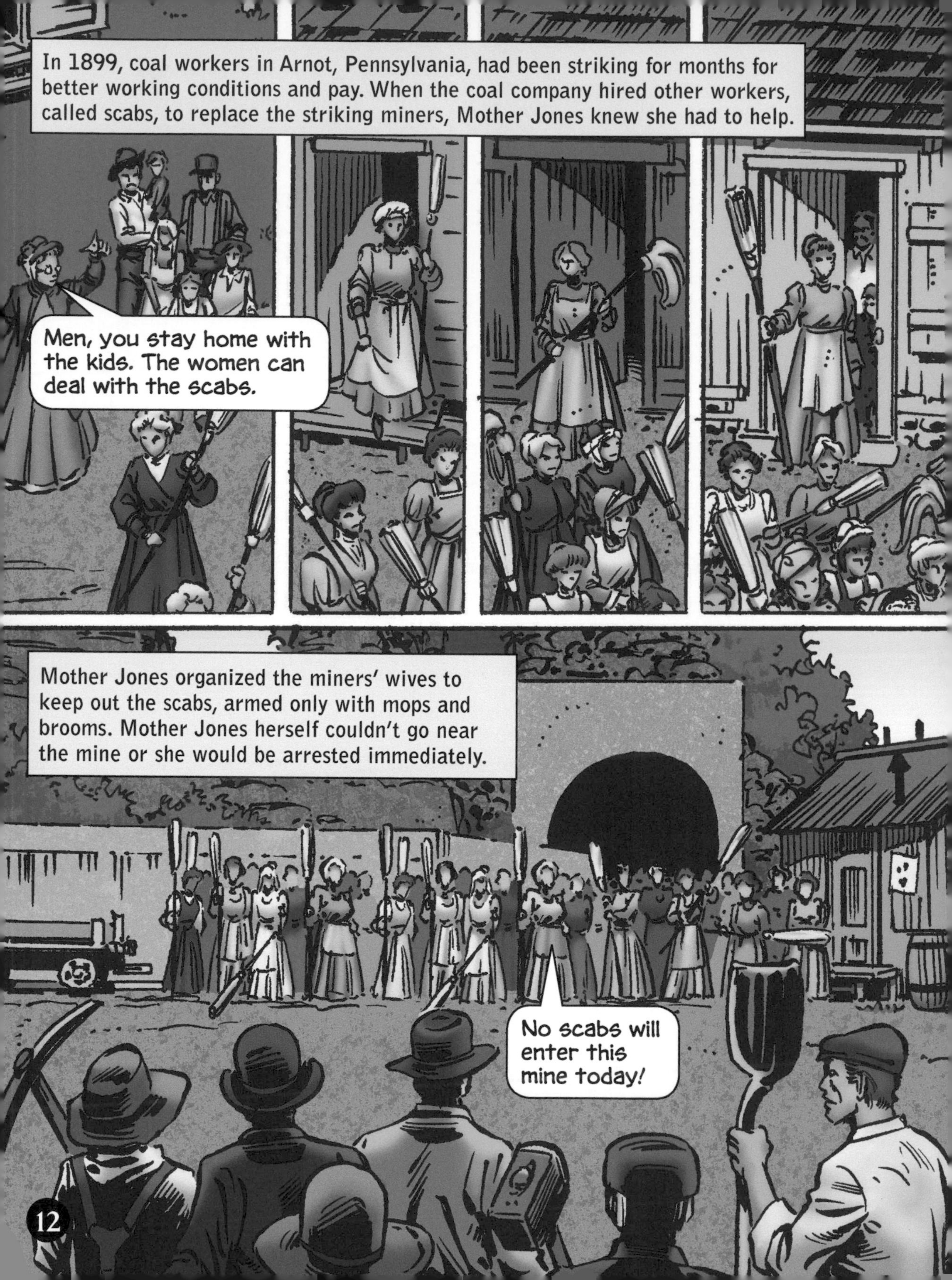
In 1899, coal workers in Arnot, Pennsylvania, had been striking for months for better working conditions and pay. When the coal company hired other workers, called scabs, to replace the striking miners, Mother Jones knew she had to help.
Men, you stay home with the kids. The women can deal with the scabs.
Mother Jones organized the miners' wives to keep out the scabs, armed only with mops and brooms. Mother Jones herself couldn't go near the mine or she would be arrested immediately.
No scabs will enter this mine today!

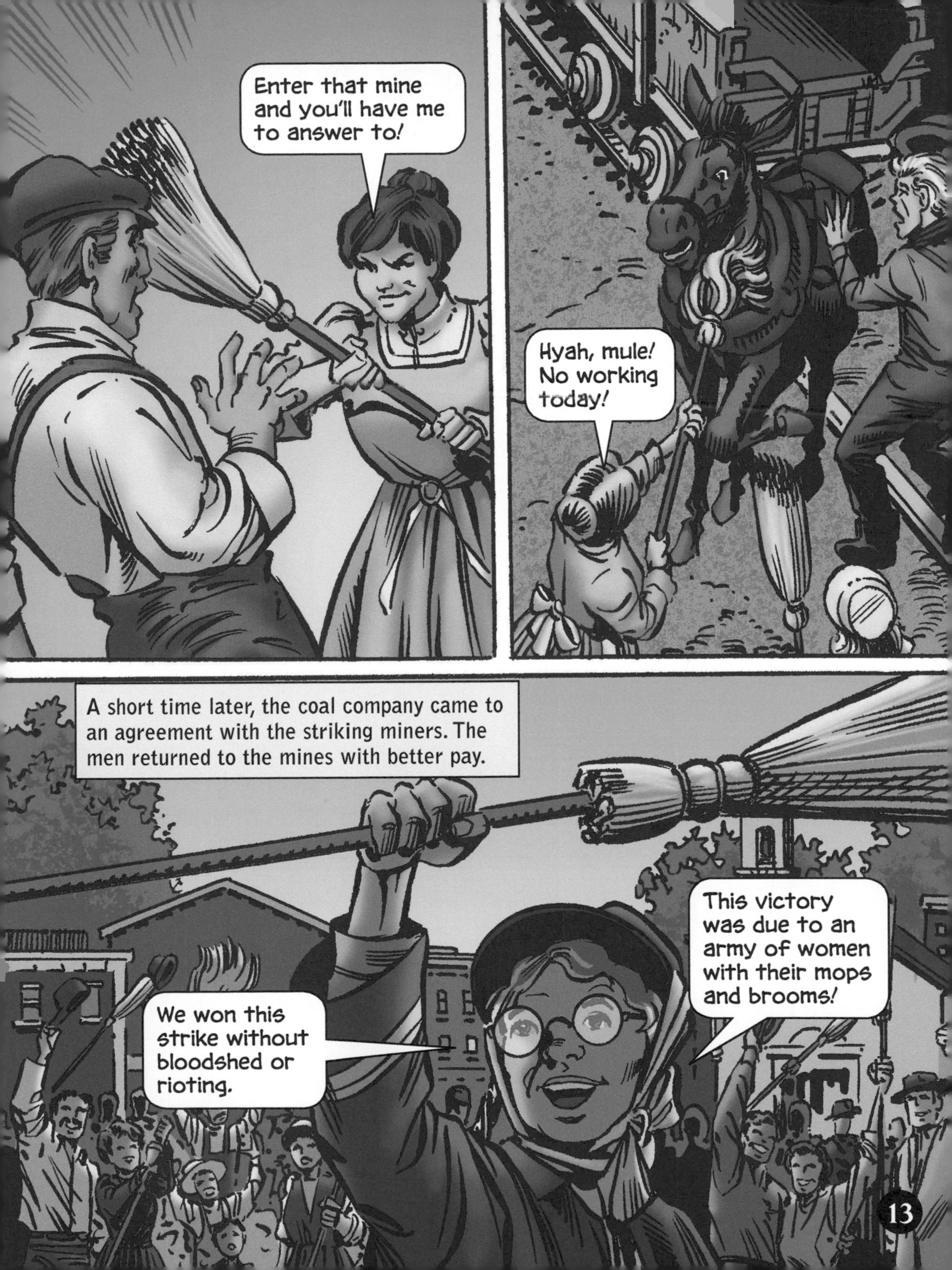

Enter that mine and you'll have me to answer to!
Hyah, mule! No working today!
A short time later, the coal company came to an agreement with the striking miners. The men returned to the mines with better pay.
We won this strike without bloodshed or rioting.
This victory was due to an army of women with their mops and brooms!

# Chapter 3
# The Working Children

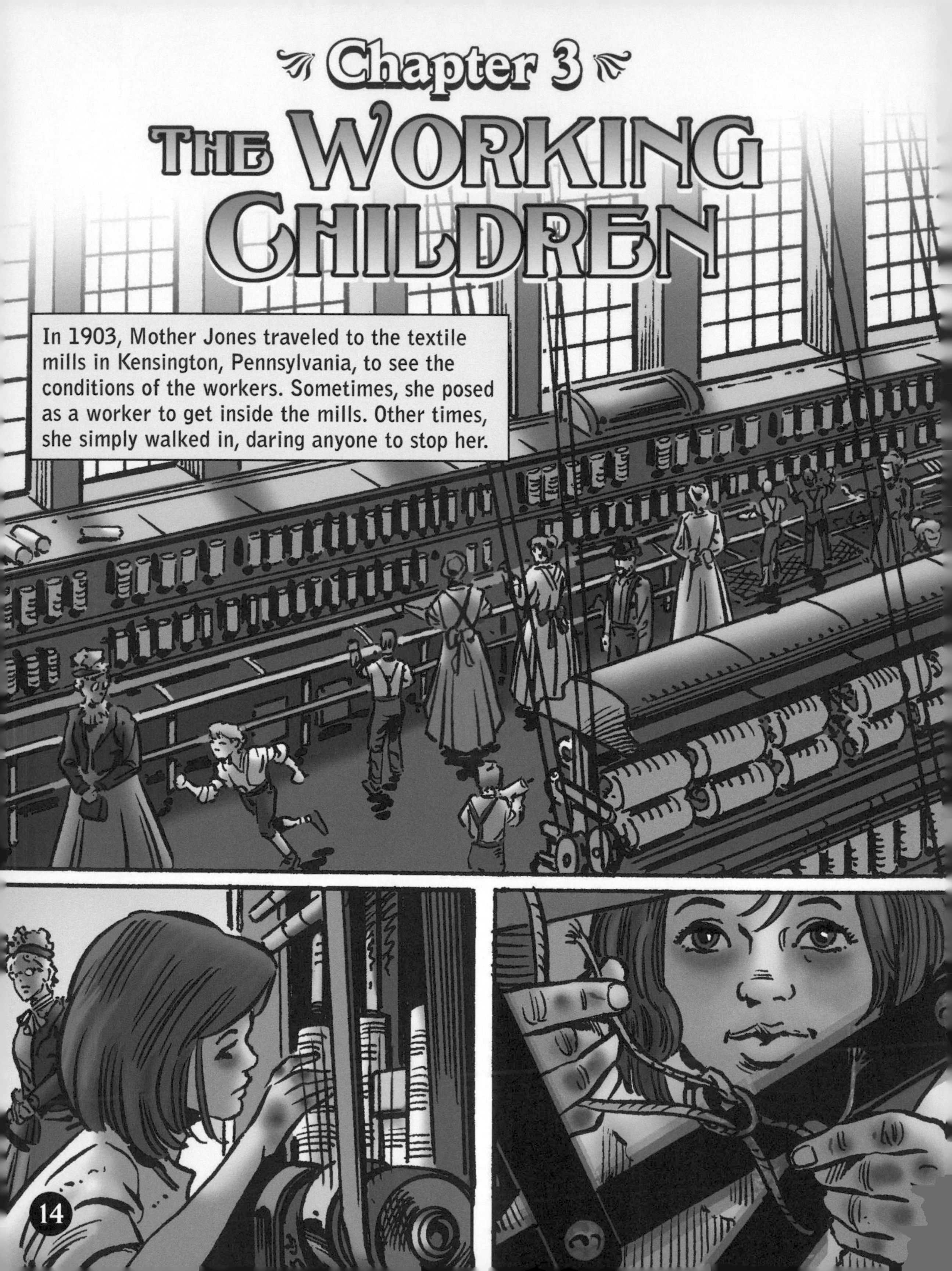
In 1903, Mother Jones traveled to the textile mills in Kensington, Pennsylvania, to see the conditions of the workers. Sometimes, she posed as a worker to get inside the mills. Other times, she simply walked in, daring anyone to stop her.

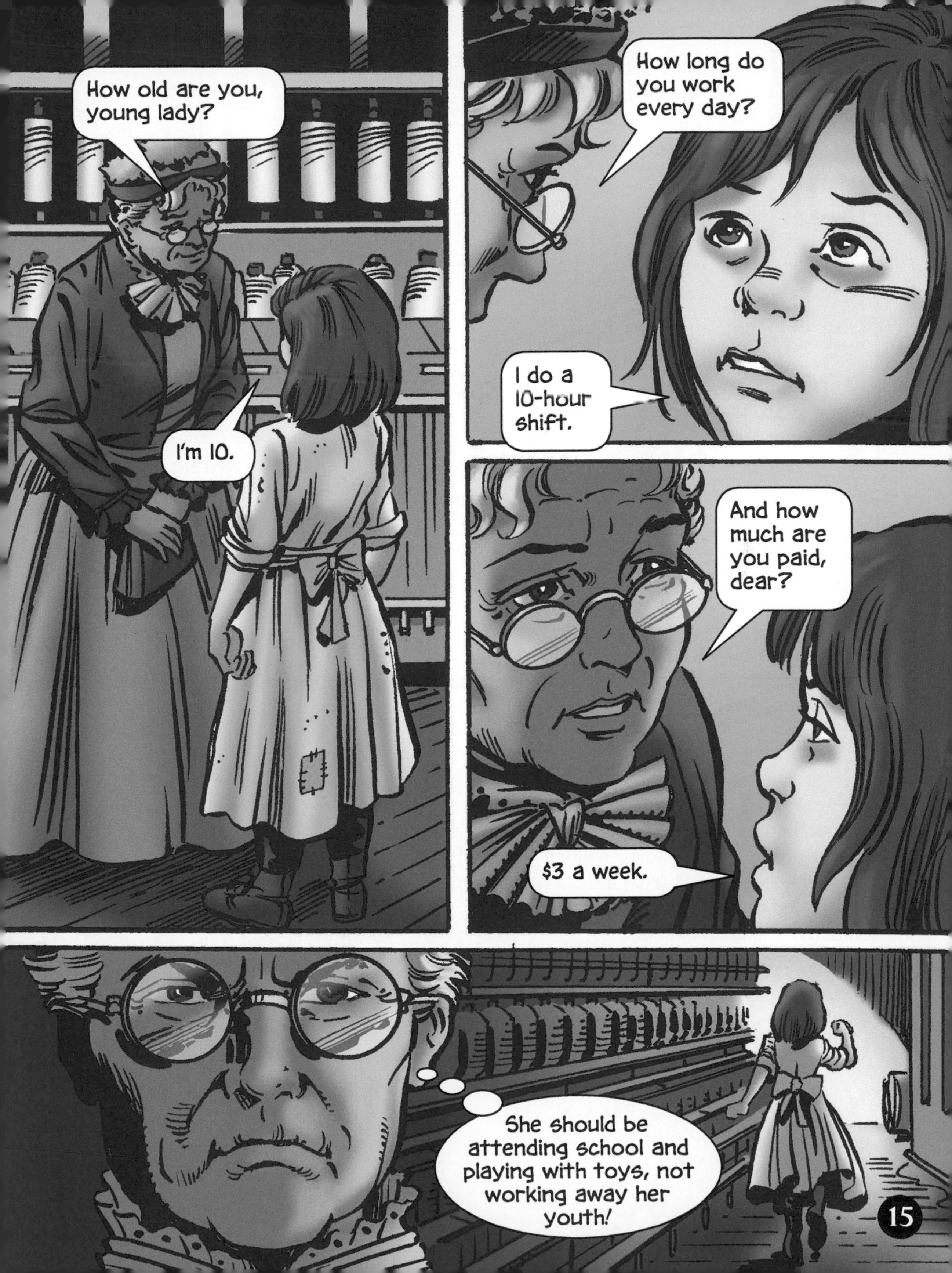
How old are you, young lady?
I'm 10.
How long do you work every day?
I do a 10-hour shift.
And how much are you paid, dear?
$3 a week.
She should be attending school and playing with toys, not working away her youth!

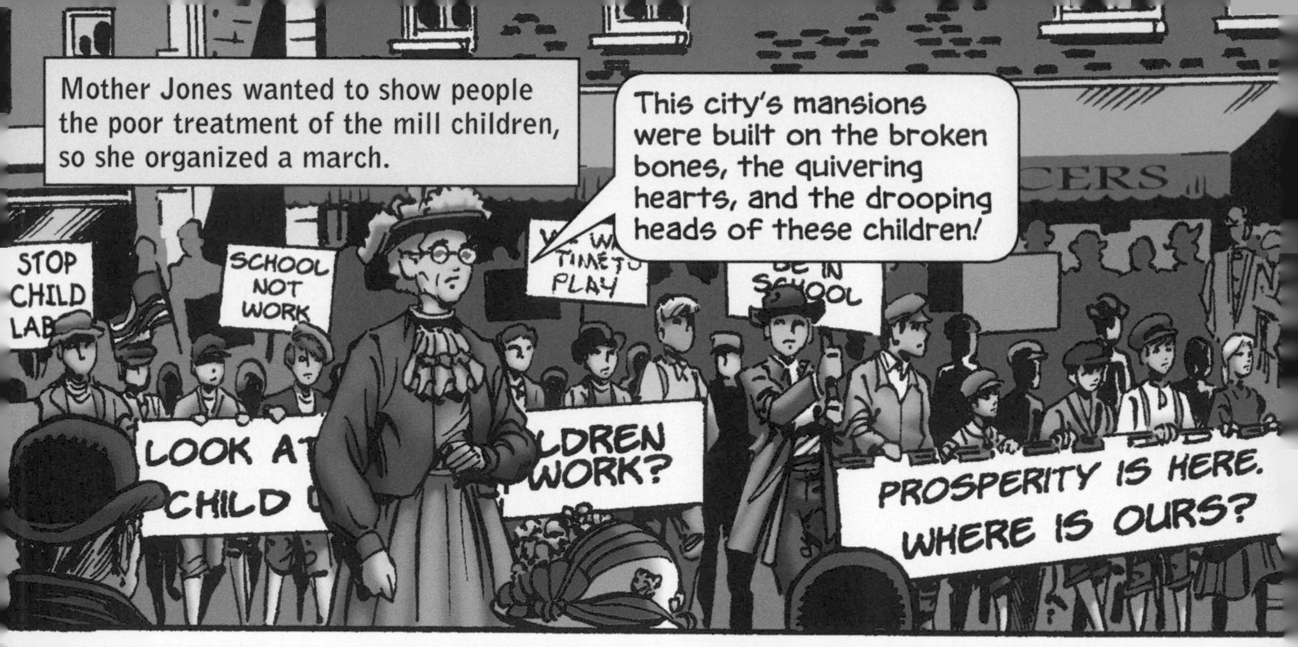
Mother Jones wanted to show people the poor treatment of the mill children, so she organized a march.
This city's mansions were built on the broken bones, the quivering hearts, and the drooping heads of these children!
STOP CHILD
SCHOOL NOT WORK
PLAY
SCHOOL
LOOK
WORK?
PROSPERITY IS HERE. WHERE IS OURS?

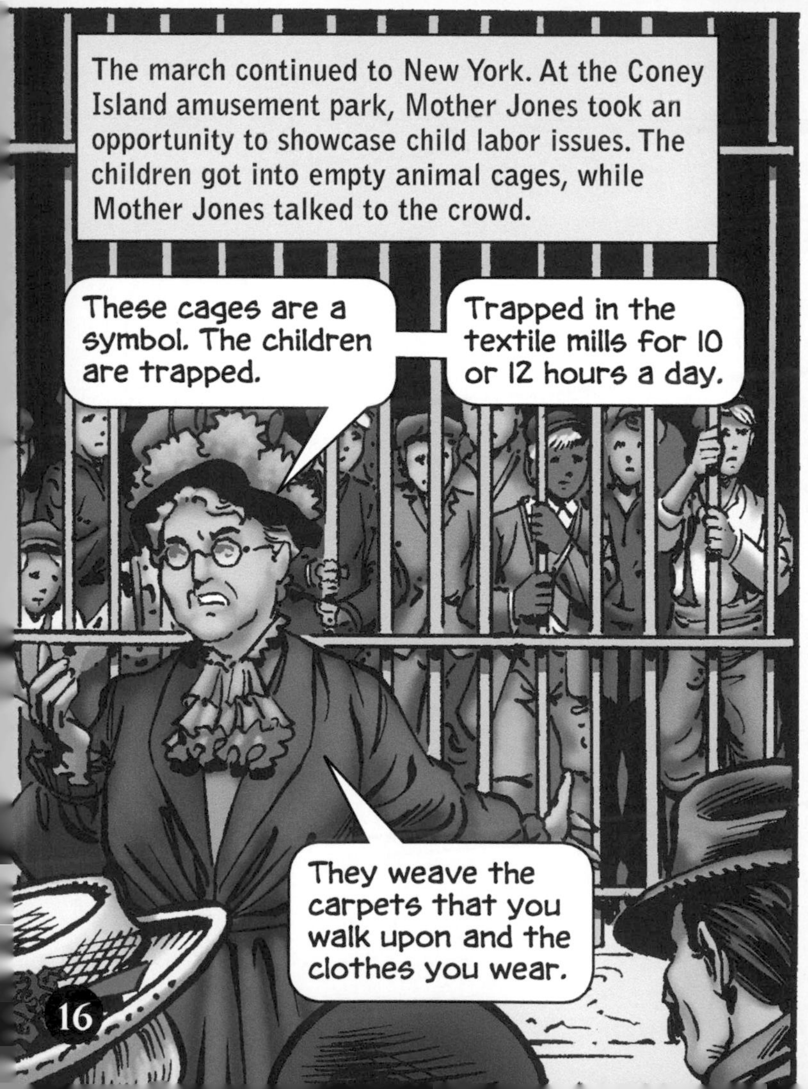
The march continued to New York. At the Coney Island amusement park, Mother Jones took an opportunity to showcase child labor issues. The children got into empty animal cages, while Mother Jones talked to the crowd.
These cages are a symbol. The children are trapped.
Trapped in the textile mills for 10 or 12 hours a day.
They weave the carpets that you walk upon and the clothes you wear.

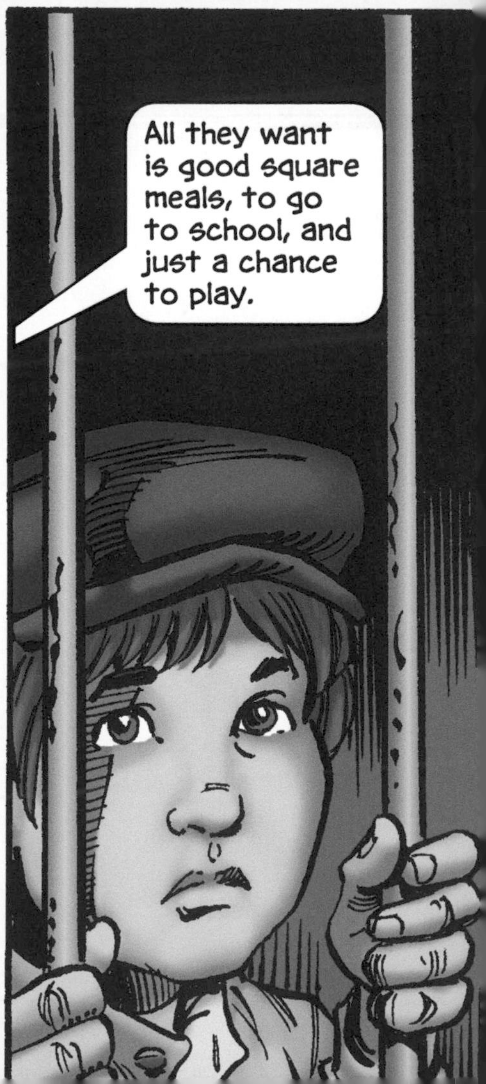
All they want is good square meals, to go to school, and just a chance to play.

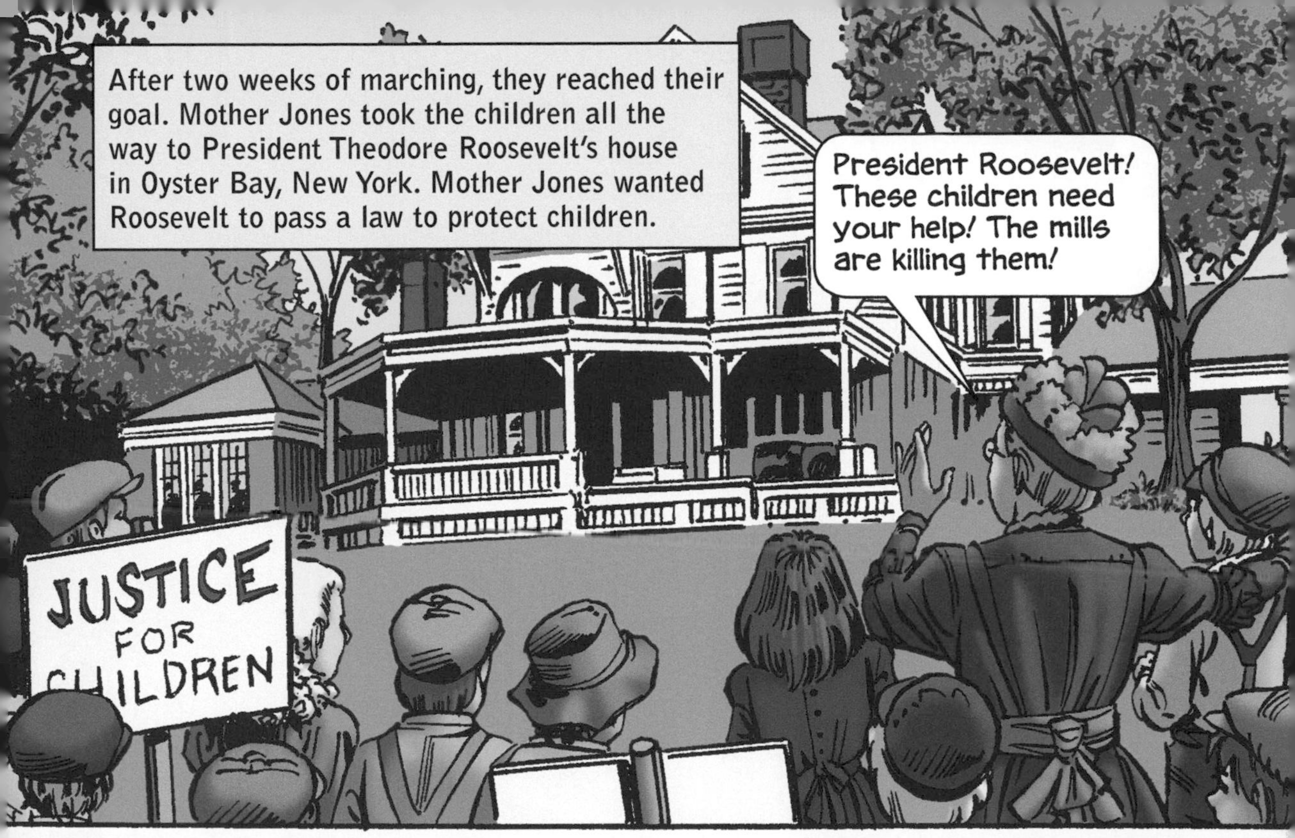
After two weeks of marching, they reached their goal. Mother Jones took the children all the way to President Theodore Roosevelt's house in Oyster Bay, New York. Mother Jones wanted Roosevelt to pass a law to protect children.
President Roosevelt! These children need your help! The mills are killing them!
JUSTICE FOR CHILDREN

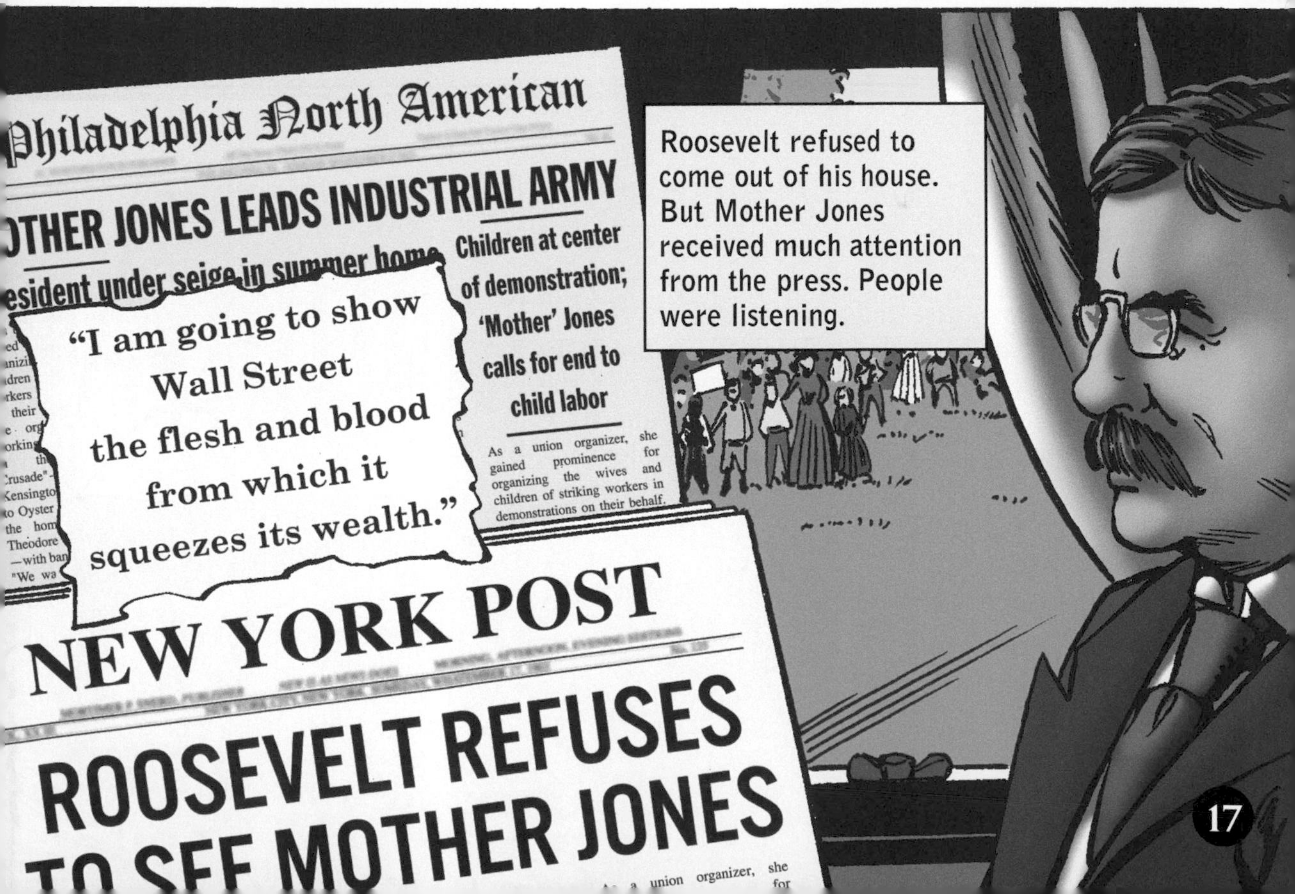
Philadelphia North American
THER JONES LEADS INDUSTRIAL ARMY
esident under seige in summer home
Children at center of demonstration; 'Mother' Jones calls for end to child labor
As a union organizer, she gained prominence for organizing the wives and children of striking workers in demonstrations on their behalf.
"I am going to show Wall Street the flesh and blood from which it squeezes its wealth."
Roosevelt refused to come out of his house. But Mother Jones received much attention from the press. People were listening.
NEW YORK POST
ROOSEVELT REFUSES
TO SEE MOTHER JONES

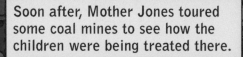

Soon after, Mother Jones toured some coal mines to see how the children were being treated there.

How old are you, lad?

Twelve, ma'am.

Why is this boy blackening his lungs at the coal mine?

His daddy is too sick to work and my job at the mill doesn't pay enough. Without my boy's pay, we would starve.

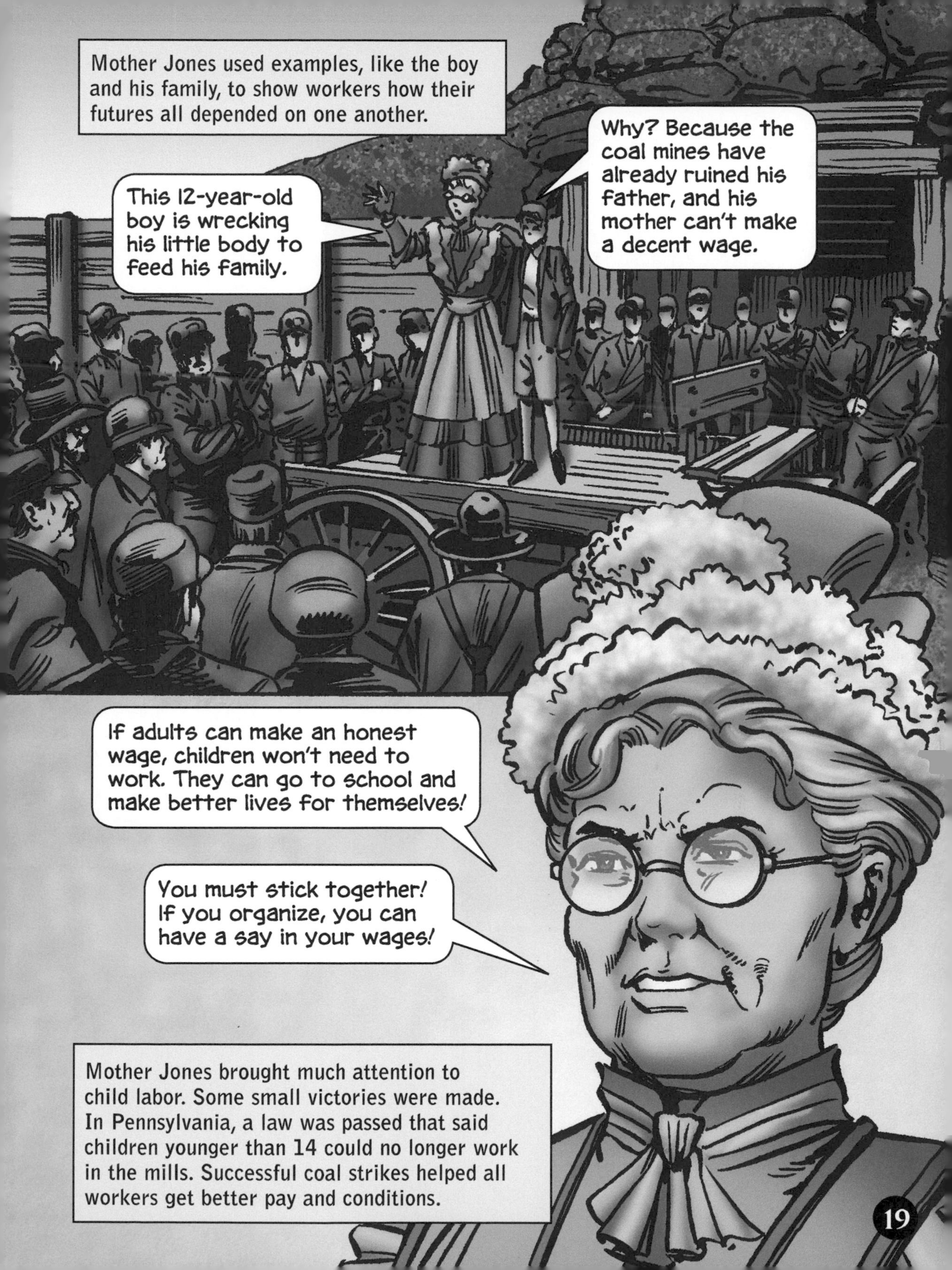
Mother Jones used examples, like the boy and his family, to show workers how their futures all depended on one another.
This 12-year-old boy is wrecking his little body to feed his family.
Why? Because the coal mines have already ruined his father, and his mother can't make a decent wage.
If adults can make an honest wage, children won't need to work. They can go to school and make better lives for themselves!
You must stick together! If you organize, you can have a say in your wages!
Mother Jones brought much attention to child labor. Some small victories were made. In Pennsylvania, a law was passed that said children younger than 14 could no longer work in the mills. Successful coal strikes helped all workers get better pay and conditions.

# Chapter 4
# THE MOST DANGEROUS WOMAN IN AMERICA

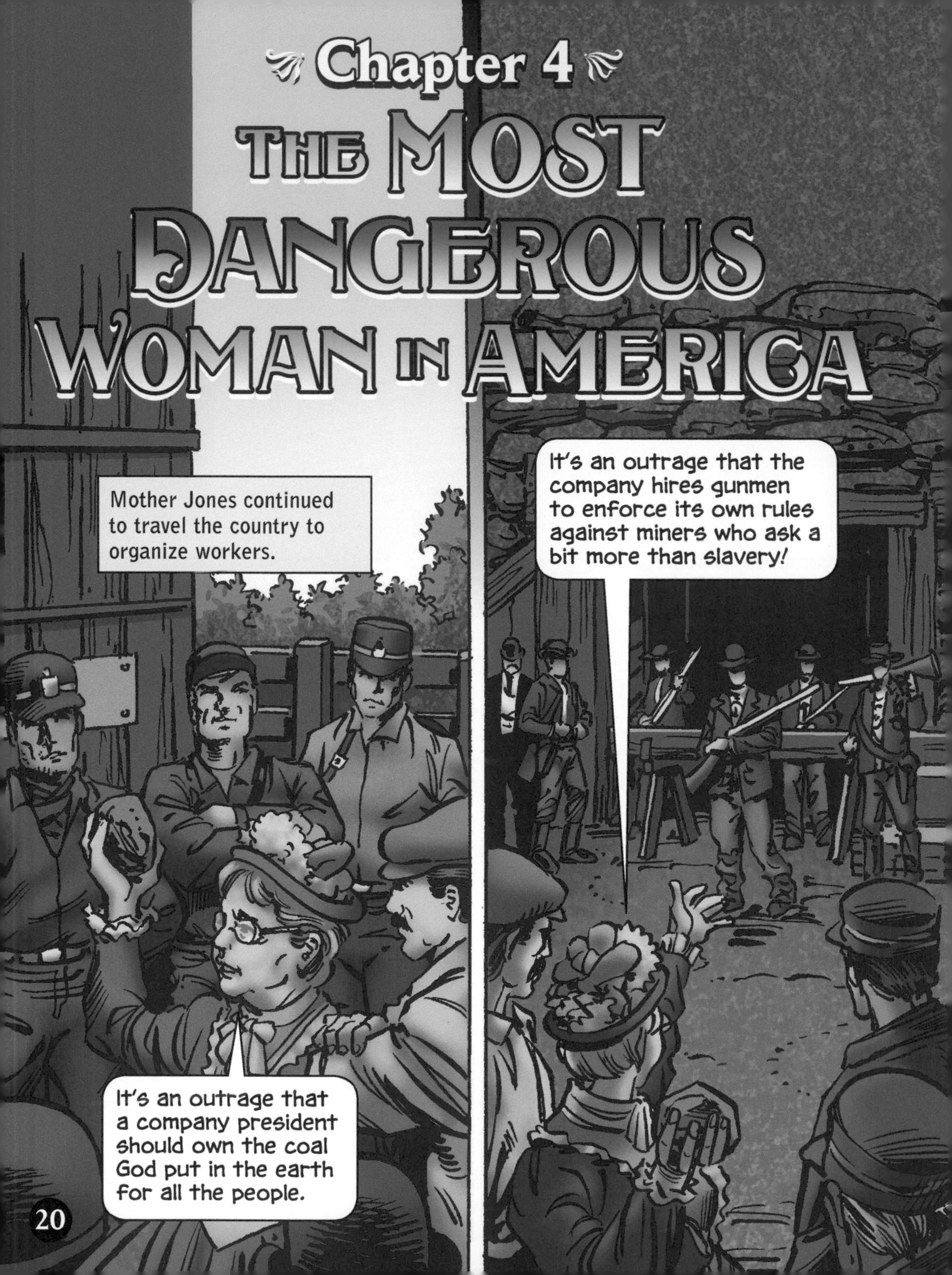
Mother Jones continued to travel the country to organize workers.
It's an outrage that a company president should own the coal God put in the earth for all the people.
It's an outrage that the company hires gunmen to enforce its own rules against miners who ask a bit more than slavery!

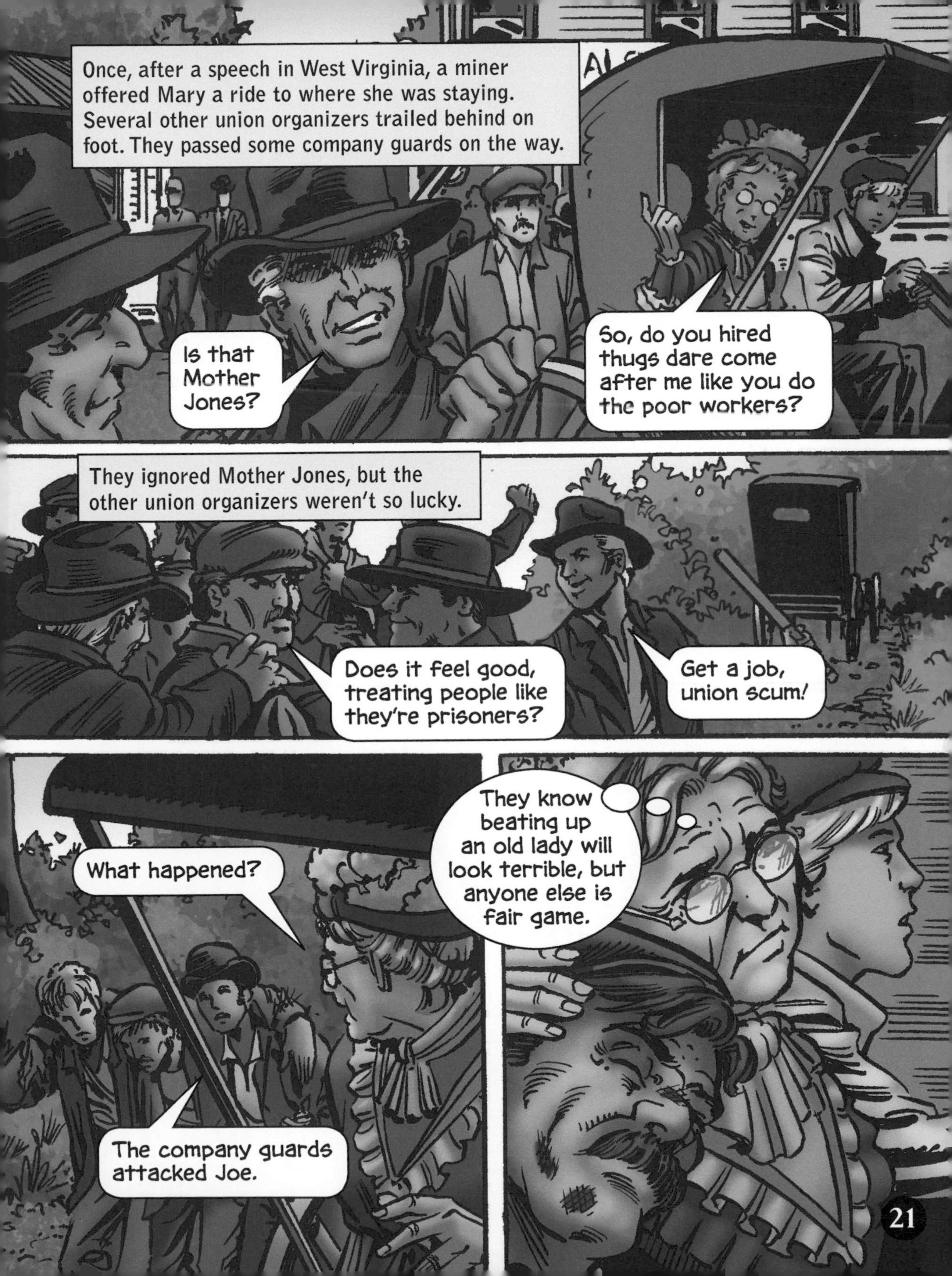
Once, after a speech in West Virginia, a miner offered Mary a ride to where she was staying. Several other union organizers trailed behind on foot. They passed some company guards on the way.
Is that Mother Jones?
So, do you hired thugs dare come after me like you do the poor workers?
They ignored Mother Jones, but the other union organizers weren't so lucky.
Does it feel good, treating people like they're prisoners?
Get a job, union scum!
What happened?
The company guards attacked Joe.
They know beating up an old lady will look terrible, but anyone else is fair game.

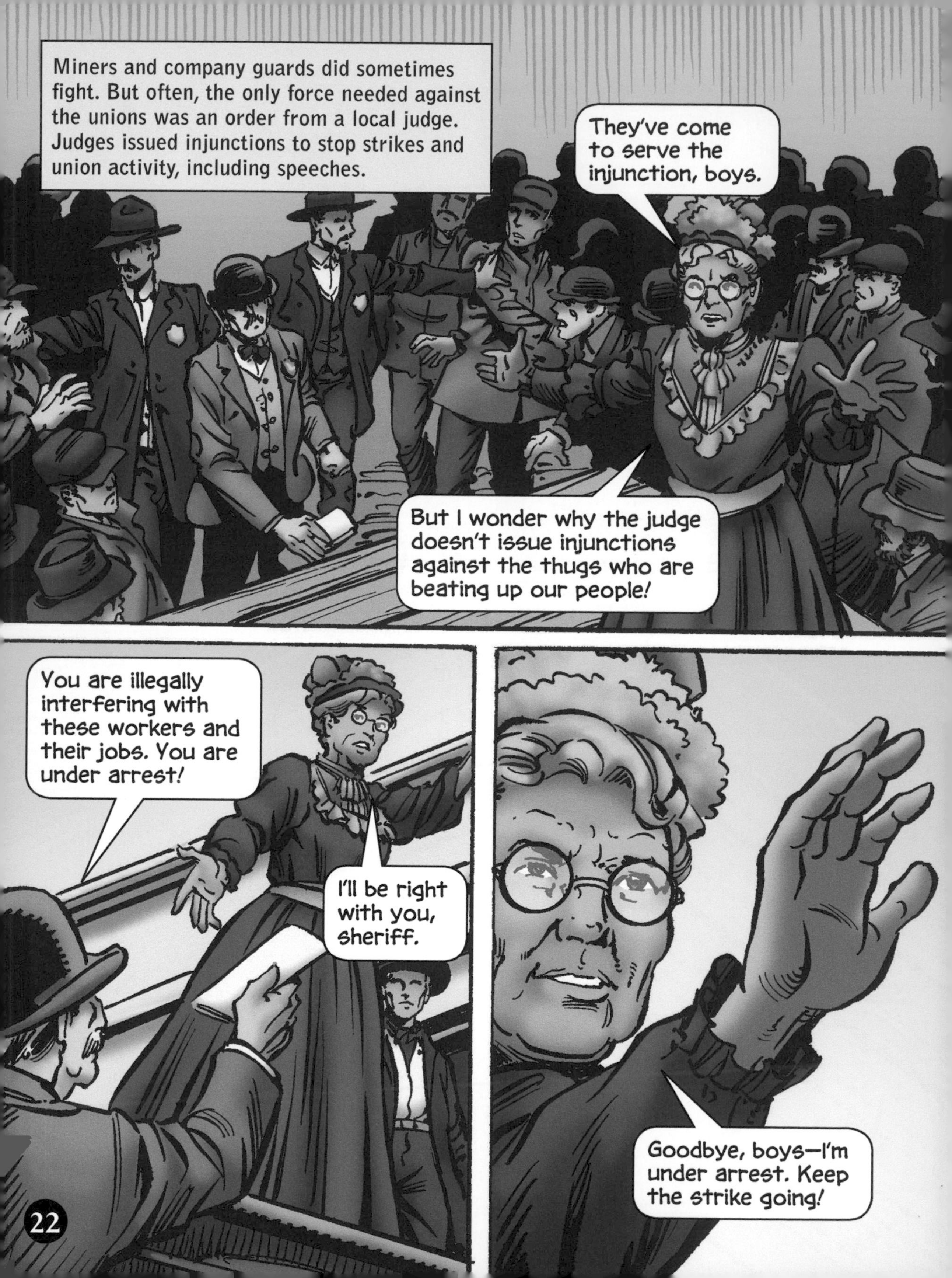
Miners and company guards did sometimes fight. But often, the only force needed against the unions was an order from a local judge. Judges issued injunctions to stop strikes and union activity, including speeches.
They've come to serve the injunction, boys.
But I wonder why the judge doesn't issue injunctions against the thugs who are beating up our people!
You are illegally interfering with these workers and their jobs. You are under arrest!
I'll be right with you, sheriff.
Goodbye, boys—I'm under arrest. Keep the strike going!

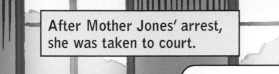

After Mother Jones' arrest, she was taken to court.

Did you intend to keep miners from going to their jobs?

Yes sir, I did. No one should work for that company in those conditions!

Your honor, there is the most dangerous woman in the country today! On her word, thousands of happy men will lay down their tools.

Go ahead, Judge, put me in jail with my men. I belong beside them.

I'm sure you'd like the publicity, but I won't let it happen. You are free to go.

I only hope someone of your intelligence will find a better use of your time than keeping men from their jobs.

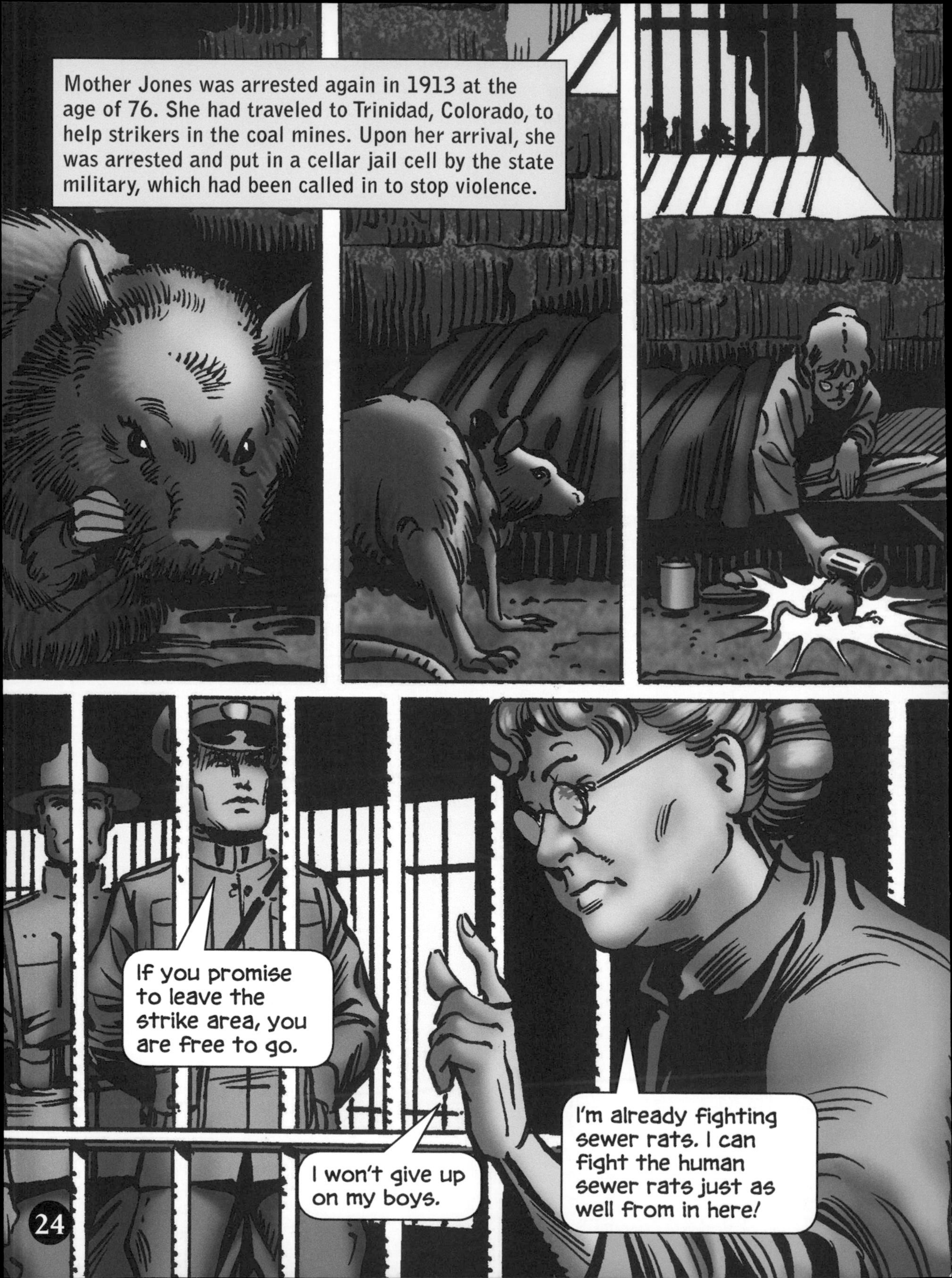

Mother Jones was arrested again in 1913 at the age of 76. She had traveled to Trinidad, Colorado, to help strikers in the coal mines. Upon her arrival, she was arrested and put in a cellar jail cell by the state military, which had been called in to stop violence.
If you promise to leave the strike area, you are free to go.
I won't give up on my boys.
I'm already fighting sewer rats. I can fight the human sewer rats just as well from in here!

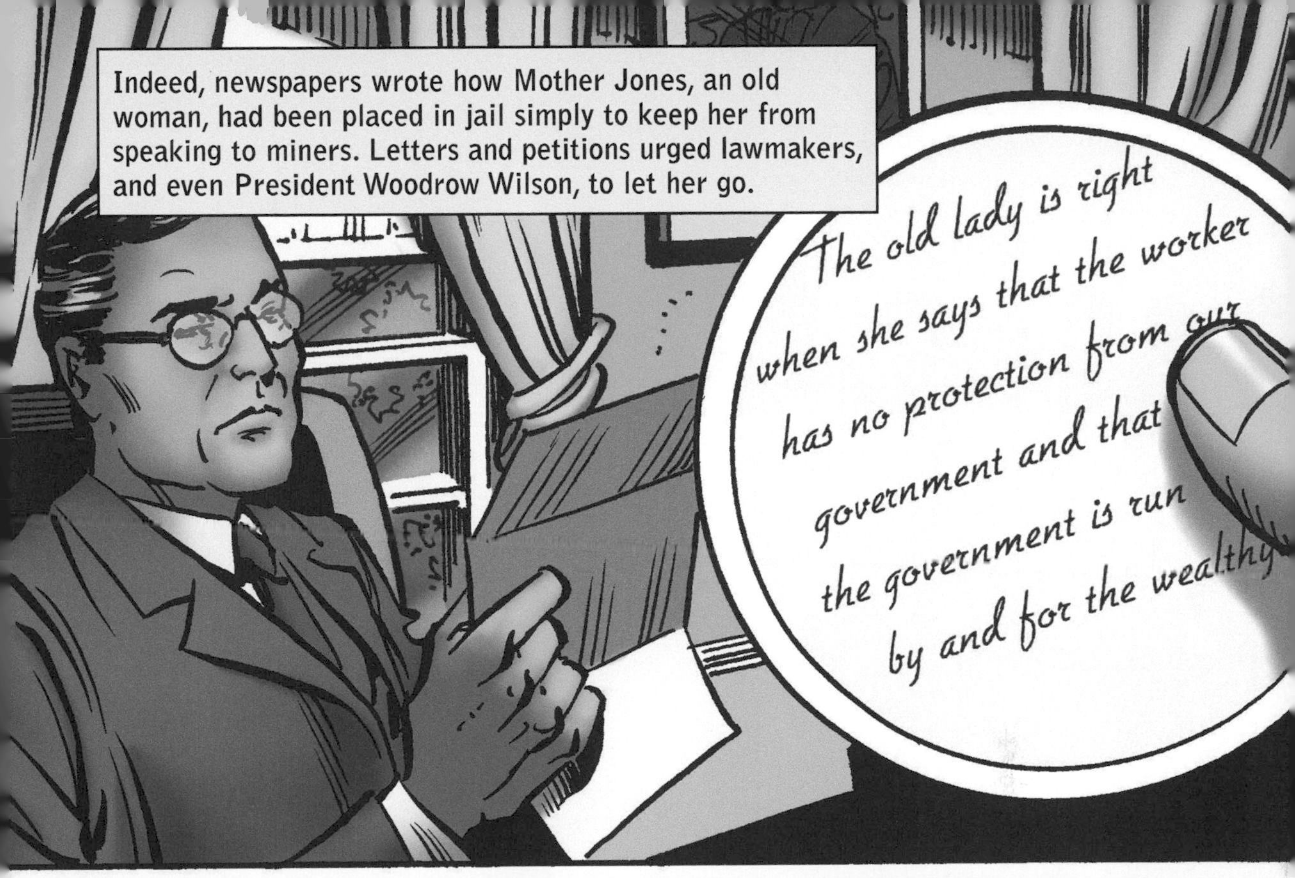
Indeed, newspapers wrote how Mother Jones, an old woman, had been placed in jail simply to keep her from speaking to miners. Letters and petitions urged lawmakers, and even President Woodrow Wilson, to let her go.
The old lady is right when she says that the worker has no protection from our government and that the government is run by and for the wealthy

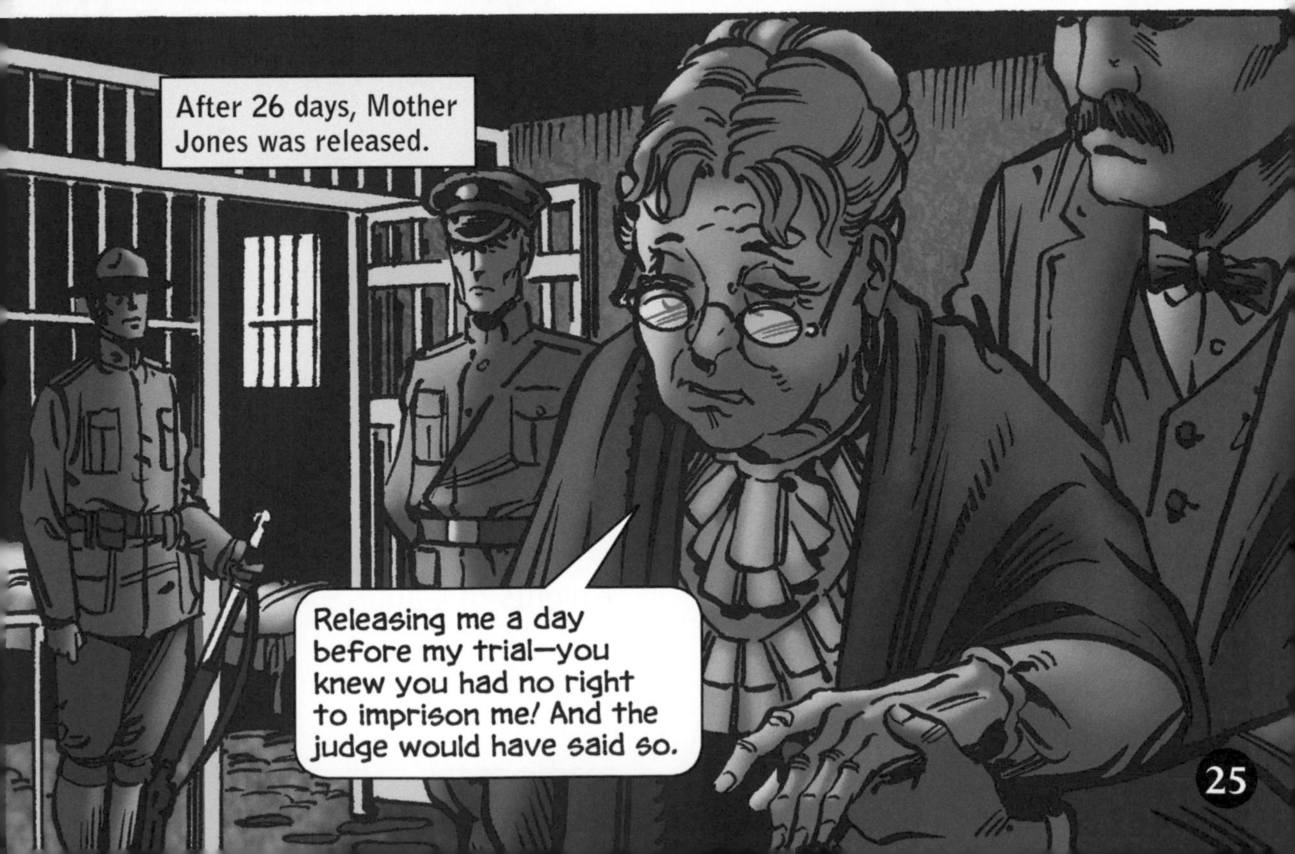
After 26 days, Mother Jones was released.
Releasing me a day before my trial—you knew you had no right to imprison me! And the judge would have said so.

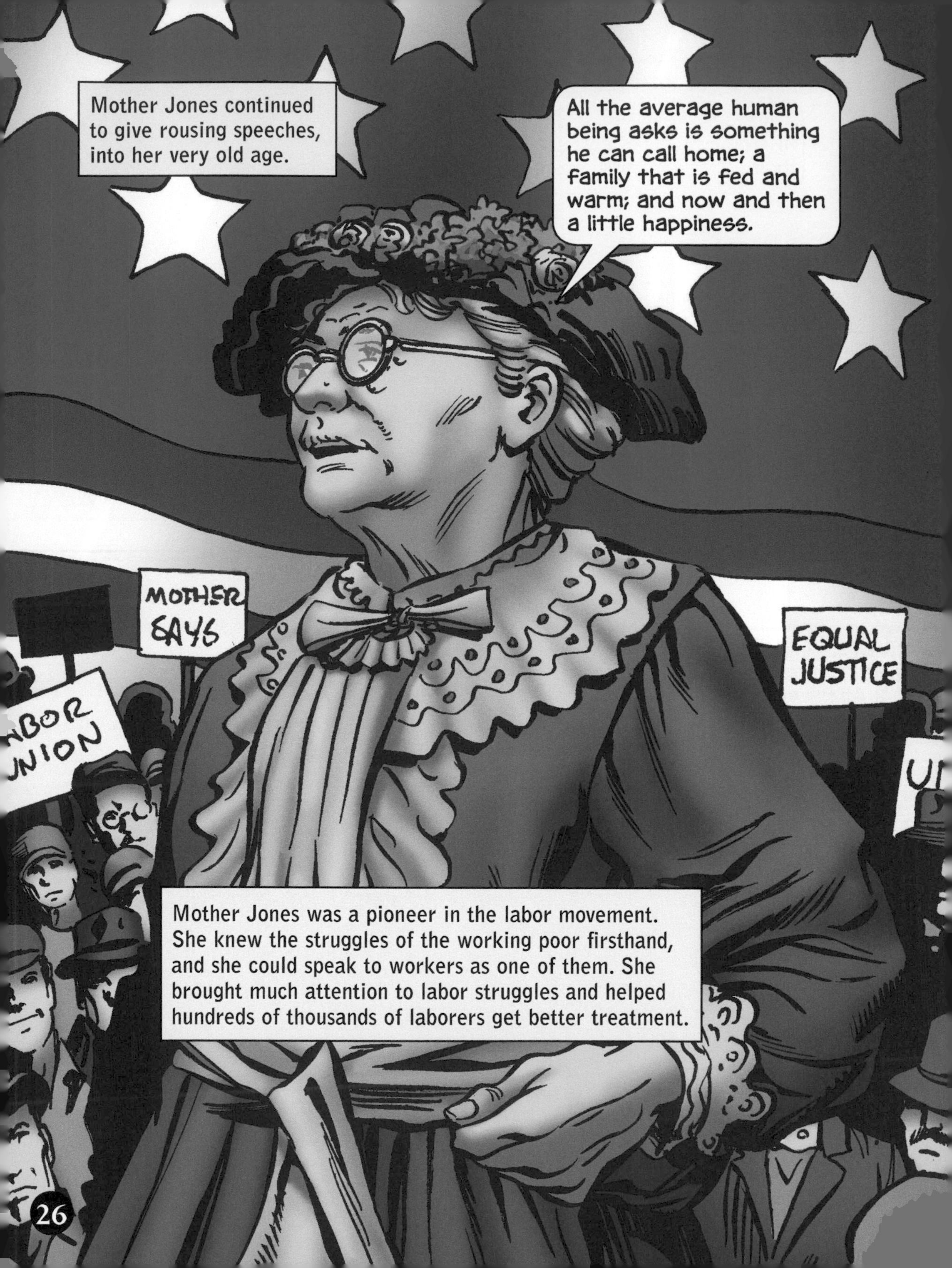
Mother Jones continued to give rousing speeches, into her very old age.
All the average human being asks is something he can call home; a family that is fed and warm; and now and then a little happiness.
MOTHER SAYS
UNION
EQUAL JUSTICE
Mother Jones was a pioneer in the labor movement. She knew the struggles of the working poor firsthand, and she could speak to workers as one of them. She brought much attention to labor struggles and helped hundreds of thousands of laborers get better treatment.

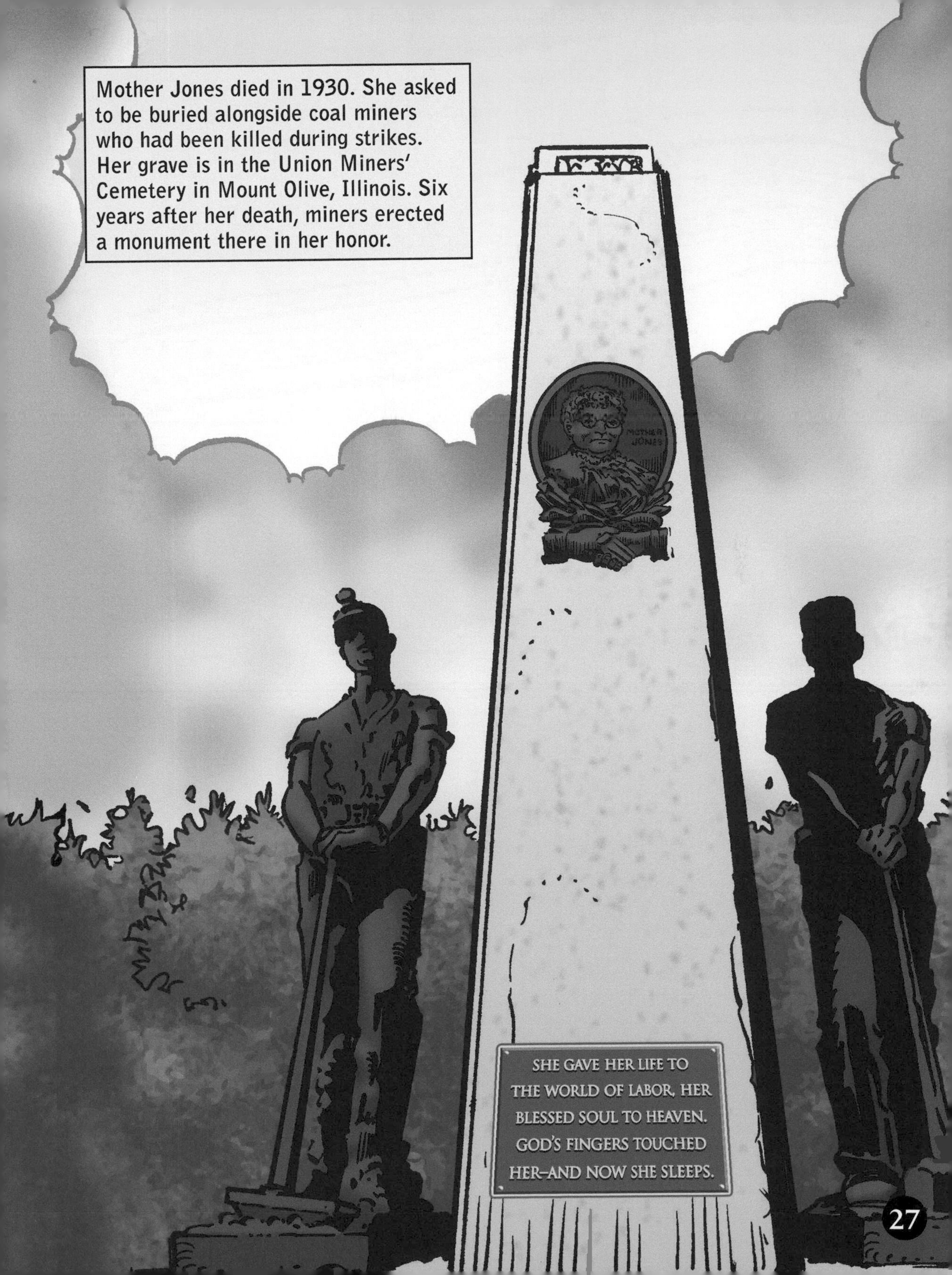
Mother Jones died in 1930. She asked to be buried alongside coal miners who had been killed during strikes. Her grave is in the Union Miners' Cemetery in Mount Olive, Illinois. Six years after her death, miners erected a monument there in her honor.
MOTHER JONES
SHE GAVE HER LIFE TO THE WORLD OF LABOR, HER BLESSED SOUL TO HEAVEN. GOD'S FINGERS TOUCHED HER–AND NOW SHE SLEEPS.

# More about MOTHER JONES

Mother Jones claimed she was born in 1830 in Cork, Ireland. Historians say she was probably born around 1837. No one knows for sure why she claimed to be older than she was.

Mother Jones also claimed May 1 as her birthday. It's unknown when her actual birthday was. May 1 was the date of the mass protest for the 8-hour work day, which she would have seen in Chicago.

Mother Jones claimed that her grandfather was hanged by British troops in Ireland for rebelling against the government. She also claimed that her father left for Canada to avoid arrest due to his rebellious activities. There's no direct evidence of these activities, but Mother Jones surely would have been aware of the problems of the Irish and their feelings toward the British.

Today, a magazine named *Mother Jones* is published. It's a non-profit magazine that aims to be a voice for social justice. It reports on social issues, including the treatment of workers today.

Mother Jones wasn't alive to see Congress pass some of the most important laws in U.S. labor history. In 1932, the Norris-LaGuardia Act barred federal court judges from issuing injunctions against labor unions. In 1938, the Fair Labor Standards Act set a minimum wage and a standard work week. It also outlawed most child labor under age 14. Children ages 14 to 16 could work only outside of school hours.

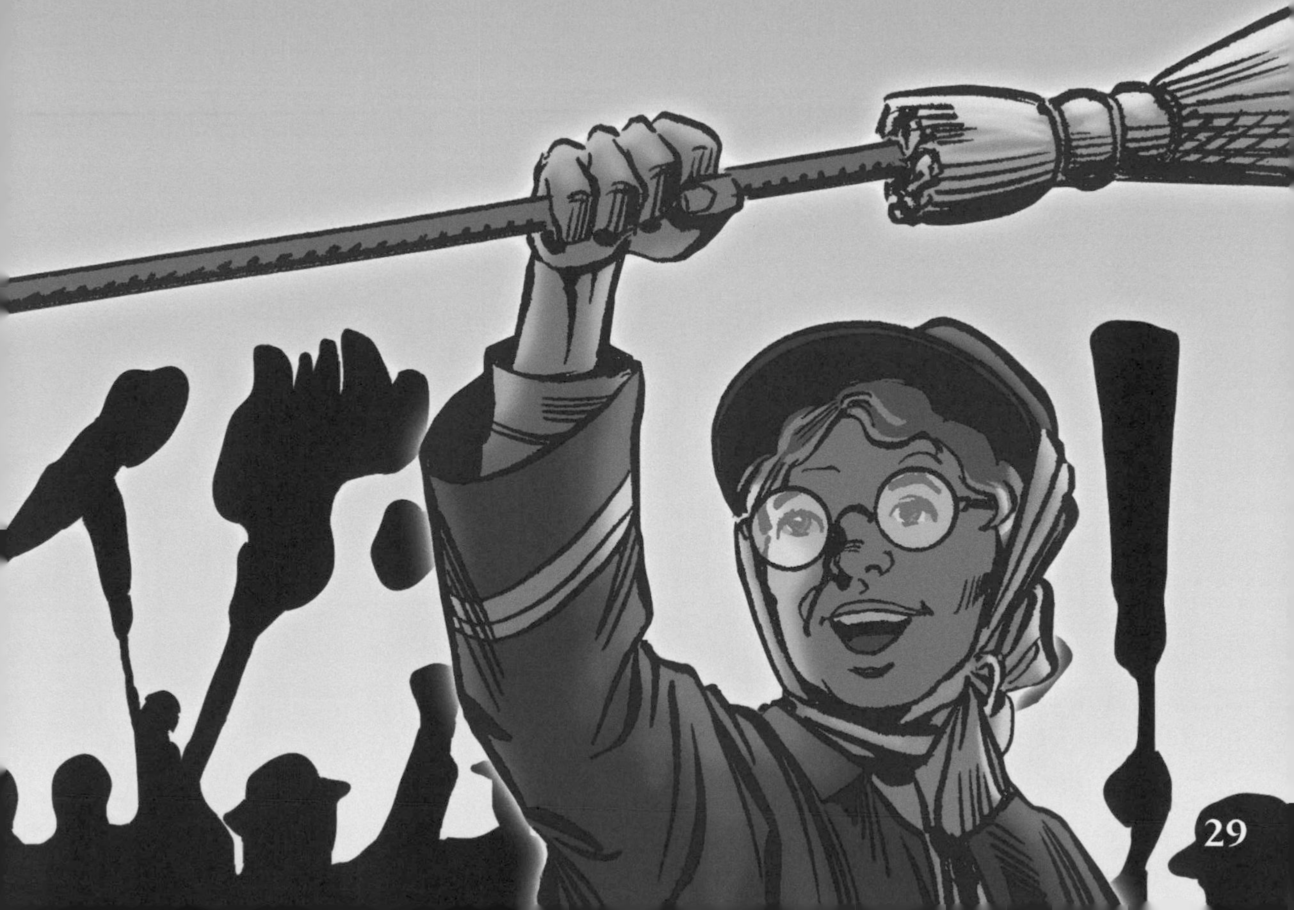

# GLOSSARY

**Industrial Revolution** (in-DUHSS-tree-uhl rev-uh-LOO-shuhn)— a period from 1790 to 1860 when work began to be done by machines, rather than by hand

**scab** (SKAB)—someone who takes the job of a union worker who is on strike

**strike** (STRIKE)—the action of refusing to work because of an argument or a disagreement with an employer over wages or working conditions

**union** (YOON-yuhn)—an organized group of workers set up to help improve such things as working conditions, wages, and health benefits

**yellow fever** (YEL-oh FEE-vur)—an illness that can cause high fever, chills, nausea, kidney and liver failure; liver failure causes the skin to become yellow, giving the disease its name.

# INTERNET SITES

FactHound offers a safe, fun way to find Internet sites related to this book. All of the sites on FactHound have been researched by our staff.

Here's how:

1. Visit *www.facthound.com*
2. Choose your grade level.
3. Type in this book ID **0736854878** for age-appropriate sites. You may also browse subjects by clicking on letters, or by clicking on pictures and words.
4. Click on the **Fetch It** button.

**FactHound will fetch the best sites for you!**

# READ MORE

Gay, Kathlyn. *Mother Jones.* Greensboro, N.C.: Morgan Reynolds, 2006.

Smith, Nigel. *The Industrial Revolution.* Events & Outcomes. Austin, Texas: Raintree Steck-Vaughn, 2003.

Woog, Adam. *A Sweatshop during the Industrial Revolution.* The Working Life. San Diego: Lucent Books, 2003.

# BIBLIOGRAPHY

Atkinson, Linda. *Mother Jones: The Most Dangerous Woman in America.* New York: Crown Publishers, 1978.

Foner, Philip S., editor. *Mother Jones Speaks: Collected Writings and Speeches.* New York: Monad Press, 1983.

Gorn, Elliott J. *Mother Jones: The Most Dangerous Woman in America.* New York: Hill and Wang, 2001.

Jones, Mary Harris. *The Autobiography of Mother Jones.* Chicago: C. H. Kerr for the Illinois Labor History Society, 1976.

# INDEX